Global Stage

Literacy Book 2

Paul Mason, Nicole Taylor, and Michael Watts

macmillan education

Scope and Sequence

Unit	Reading 1	Reading 2	Reading Skill	Content Area	Social and Emotional Learning	Key Concept	Language Book
Phonics Review	Long vowel sounds, blends and digraphs, CVC words						
1 What Does It Do? page 8	**Fiction** *The After-School Inventor* Story *cl–* blend	**Nonfiction** *My Good Ideas Book* Instructional Text	Identifying a Sequence of Events	Science Technology	Self-Awareness Accurately recognize own strengths and limitations	Why do people invent things?	**Vocabulary** gadgets, places and objects in school **Grammar** simple present with adverbs of frequency present progressive review
2 Thank You page 24	**Nonfiction** *Chuseok: Korea's Harvest Festival* Informational Text	**Fiction** *First Harvest* Science Fiction –st blend	Under-standing the Setting	Social Studies Communities	Self-Awareness Identify what triggers emotions	Why do we celebrate harvests?	**Vocabulary** food, containers, food and drink **Grammar** quantifiers with statements and questions
3 It Keeps Changing page 40	**Fiction** *The Bear and I* Poem –*ng* blend	**Nonfiction** *Clean Cars* Informational Text	Comparing and Contrasting Information	Science Environmental Science	Social Awareness Evaluate others' emotional reactions	How can we make good changes in our world?	**Vocabulary** nature and animals **Grammar** simple past: *be*
4 What Happened? page 56	**Nonfiction** *Where Is She?* Informational Text	**Fiction** *The Angry Mountain* Story –*nd* blend	Identifying a Cause and Effect	History World Events	Self-Awareness Label and recognize emotions	How do events change our lives?	**Vocabulary** action verbs **Grammar** simple past: regular verbs
5 Let's Go Back page 72	**Fiction** *The Time Book* Fantasy	**Nonfiction** *Time Capsules* Informational Text –*nt* blend	Identifying the Main Idea and Details	History Civilizations	Social Awareness Understand other views and perspectives	How can we find out about the past?	**Vocabulary** parts of the body, adjectives, fossils, and ruins **Grammar** simple past: irregular verbs

Unit	Reading 1	Reading 2	Reading Skill	Content Area	Social and Emotional Learning	Key Concept	Language Book
6 Look What I Made page 88	**Fiction** *The Superstar* Story *wh–* digraph	**Nonfiction** *Visit Gaudí's World* Informational Text	Identifying Fact and Opinion	Science Architecture	Self-Management Set plans and work towards goals	Why do people make things?	**Vocabulary** art, physical characteristics, and short adjectives **Grammar** comparatives: short adjectives superlatives: short adjectives
7 We're a Team page 104	**Nonfiction** *Great Teamwork* Informational Text	**Fiction** *It's Mine* Story *–ck* blend	Predicting Endings	Science Symbiotic Relationships	Relationship Skills Exhibit cooperative learning and working towards group goals	What is good about teamwork?	**Vocabulary** activities and working with others **Grammar** telling the time modal verbs: *can* for permissions, requests, and offers
8 You're My Hero page 120	**Nonfiction** *In First Place* Biography	**Fiction** *A New Hero* Play *tr–* blends	Understanding Characters	History Important People	Responsible Decision-Making Identify problems when making decisions and generate alternatives	What makes a hero?	**Vocabulary** sports, long adjectives, and attributes **Grammar** comparatives: long adjectives superlatives: long adjectives
9 Do You Live Here? page 136	**Fiction** *The Clever King* Fable	**Nonfiction** *Amazing Castles* Informational Text *br–* blend	Scanning for Specific Information	Science Architecture	Self-Management Regulate emotions such as impulses, aggression, and self-destructive behavior	Why did people build castles?	**Vocabulary** around the home and emotions **Grammar** simple past review *there was / there were*
10 Are We There Yet? page 152	**Fiction** *Young Nicholas* Story *sw–* blend	**Nonfiction** *The Thirty-Year Journey* Biography	Identifying the Sequence of Events	History Important People	Self-Management Display grit, determination, or perseverance	Why do people travel?	**Vocabulary** journeys and weather **Grammar** future plans: *going to* prepositions of movement

A Listen and say. Then look at the pictures and write the words with the long *a* sound.

1 
cake

2 

3 

4 

5 

6 

7 

8 

B Listen and say. Then choose the words with the long *e* sound.

1	bed	(tree)	red
2	pretty	teeth	net
3	hen	leg	green
4	sweet	pen	chef
5	nest	eat	peg
6	bee	desk	egg
7	these	elephant	help
8	mess	get	leaf

C Listen and say. Then complete the words with the long *u* sound.

1 gl u e
2 c __ t __
3 j __ __ ce
4 T __ __ sday
5 bl __ __
6 fr __ __ t
7 s __ __ p
8 r __ __ m

D Listen and say. Choose the letters that make the long *i* sound. Then complete the table.

1 Friday
2 kind
3 nine
4 bike
5 ice
6 lion
7 climb
8 drive

i	i_e
Friday	

E Listen and say. Then complete the sentences using a word with the long *o* sound.

soap goat bowl ~~boat~~ yellow toe hippo sofa

1 The ___boat___ sailed on the water.
2 The farmer had a ________ .
3 The girl ate a ________ of cereal.
4 Grandma smelled the ________ flower.
5 Use ________ to wash your hands.
6 The ________ stays in the water all day.
7 She is sitting on the ________ .
8 Ow! I hit my ________ .

F Match the words to the correct long vowel sound.

cold	long e	main
five	long *a*	you
oops	long *i*	line
way	long *u*	green
toe	long o	teach

A Listen and choose the correct word with *sh*.

1 On the beach, we find shells / shirts.
2 There is a trash / fish in the sea.
3 Put on your shoes / shell.
4 Remember to wash / push your hands before lunch.
5 Please shower / shut the door.
6 Her shout / shirt is yellow.
7 I brush / push my teeth in the morning.
8 His hair is very shoe / short.

B Listen and say. Use *st* or *ch* to complete the words. Then match.

a 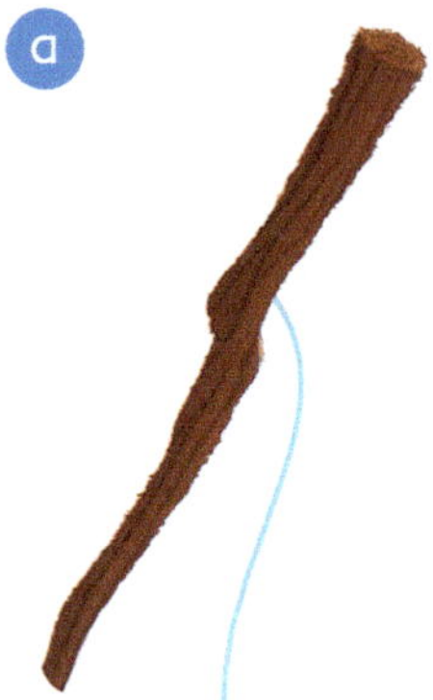

b 

c 

d 

1 st ick
2 ____ air
3 ____ rawberries
4 ____ eck
5 ____ ar
6 ____ icken
7 ____ orm
8 ____ ild

e 

f 

g 

h 

C Unscramble these words starting with *pl* or *fl*.

1 anplt plant
4 lpum ______
7 erfolw ______
2 lapf ______
5 tolaf ______
8 ypal ______
3 yfl ______
6 plena ______
9 lteap ______

D Listen and say. Then listen again and write the words starting with *pr* or *fr*.

1 prize
2 ______
3 ______
4 ______
5 ______
6 ______
7 ______
8 ______
9 ______

E Find the words with blends and digraphs.

plate pretty fries chair float stand shirt

F	C	H	E	S	S	S	P
R	S	T	A	N	D	L	L
I	W	F	G	P	W	U	A
E	P	L	C	Y	S	G	T
S	X	O	H	C	H	B	E
R	X	A	A	Z	I	M	F
E	L	T	I	F	R	U	X
B	W	P	R	E	T	T	Y

UNIT 1

What Does It Do?

See, Think, Wonder

A Look at the picture. What do you see?

I see a lamp.

There's a small robot.

B What do you think?

I think the books are old.

He's smart.

C What do you wonder?

Is it night?

How old is the robot?

D Think and discuss. What do inventors do?

E Think and discuss. Which of these things do you think inventors do first? Check (✔).

1 Draw a picture. ◯

2 Make changes. ◯

3 Have ideas. ◯

Now read **The After-School Inventor**

The After-School Inventor

My name is Clara Doodle.
I invent things after school.

I have a lot of new ideas and some of them are cool.

Are all of Clara's inventions good?

Words in Context

Find these words in the reading. What do you think they mean?

invent try again change mirror mess invention machine

When I have an idea, I always make a plan.

I draw and change, and change and draw. I do the best I can.

eraser
rubber

Look at the buttons on the mirror. What things can the mirror do?

Which invention is your favorite?

US	UK
clean	tidy
favorite	favourite

Explore the Reading

A Read and match.

1 This invention cleans.
2 This invention has buttons.
3 This invention is for the rain.
4 This invention helps Clara with her homework.
5 This invention sings a song.

a. the pen umbrella
b. the alarm clock pillow
c. the smart eraser
d. the clean-up machine
e. the mirror

B Read and choose the answer.

The mirror doesn't work. She tries again.
~~She invents things after school.~~ Her mom does.
It cleans her room. She makes a plan.

1 When does Clara invent things? She invents things after school.
2 What does she do if her idea is not very good? ______
3 What does she do when she has a new idea? ______
4 Why does Clara say "Oh, no!"? ______
5 Who thinks Clara's room is a mess? ______
6 What does her new invention do? ______

C Think and discuss. Do you think it is easy or difficult to be an inventor? Why?

I think it's difficult because you have to work hard.

Phonics *cl–*

Listen and say.

climb clue cloud close clap

Now find more words starting with *cl–* in the reading.

A Look and read. Then write the instructions in order.

Press play. **Type password.** **Play the game.** **Press on.**

Some readings give us instructions. This information has an order. This **sequence** helps us learn how to do something.

B Read and put in order.

First **Second** **Third** **Last**

__________, an inventor makes the invention.

__________, an inventor has a good idea for an invention.

__________, an inventor tests the invention.

__________, an inventor writes down the plan for the invention.

C Think and discuss. Why do you think inventors have notebooks?

It's because they want to remember things.

Now read **My Good Ideas Book**

MY GOOD IDEAS BOOK

1 Get started.

Write your ideas down.
A lot of them!
Choose a good one.

Thomas Edison (1847–1931)
Inventions: movie projector, sound recorder, light bulb

When you have a problem, look for a solution.

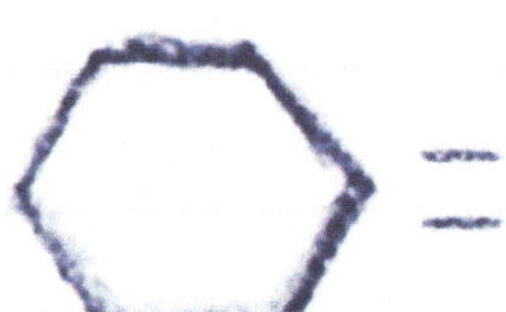

Thomas Edison had thousands of notebooks.

This plant sticks to your clothes.

This shoe sticks like the plant.

Look at animals and plants. They can give you good ideas.

Where do new ideas come from?

Kingfishers fly fast.

This train's shape is like the kingfisher.

old + old + old = new

Words in Context

Find these words in the reading. What do you think they mean?

problem **solution** **hexagon** **improve** **parachute**

2 Work on your idea.

Draw a picture of your idea. Drawing helps you to see your idea. When you see a problem, you can change it.

Leonardo da Vinci (1452–1519)
Ideas: a parachute, a helicopter, a flying machine

3 Improve your idea.

Show your idea to your friends and family.
Listen to what they say and maybe change your idea.

Karl Benz (1844–1929) invented the first motorcar in 1885.

Do you like drawing or making new things?

Don't give up! → Try again ... → and again ... → and again!

Explore the Reading

A Read and put in order.

make a drawing | share your idea | ~~try again~~ | have a good idea | draw a picture

1. ______________
2. ______________
3. ______________
4. ______________
5. try again

B Read and complete.

1. **To make a Good Ideas Book you need ...**
   - ideas
   - ______________
   - ______________
   - a pencil

2. **To get new ideas, you can think about ...**
   - a problem
   - objects you use
   - ______________
   - ______________

3. **When you have a new idea ...**
   - write it down
   - ______________
   - test your idea
   - improve your idea
   - ______________

C Think and discuss. How are these inventions helpful?

parachutes | trains | pencils | light bulbs

Parachutes are helpful so you can be safe.

Why do people invent things?

A Read and match the inventions to the inventors. Complete the Invention column.

the parachute the movie projector
the alarm clock pillow the car

Inventor	Invention	Reason
Clara Doodle		
Karl Benz		
Leonardo da Vinci		
Thomas Edison		

B Look at A. What is the reason for each invention?
Complete the Reason column.

to travel in the air to wake up on time
to travel quickly with no horses to show movies

C Think and share. Why are these inventions important? Give reasons.
Do a Round Robin.

robot TV computer glass

My Reading Journal

Write three interesting things from this unit.

1 ______________________________

2 ______________________________

3 ______________________________

What's an invention you want to know about? How can you learn about it?

I want to know about ______________________________.

I can learn about it by ______________________________.

UNIT 2

Thank You

Think, Pair, Share

A Look at the picture. Why are they holding these things? Think about it.

B Talk with your partner.

What do you think?

I think that's his home.

C Share with the class.

We think he's thankful for his home.

D Think and discuss. When do you say "thank you"?

E Look at the picture. Where do you think it is?

Now read **Chuseok: Korea's Harvest Festival**

Nonfiction

Chuseok:
Korea's Harvest Festival

Who can weave the most cloth? Two teams have a contest to find out. They weave and weave for a whole month!

It is the night of the full moon. The king comes. "This team wins!" he says. The prize is a big feast for both teams. Some people say this is the beginning of the *Chuseok* holiday.

Today, the festival of *Chuseok* is still an important holiday in Korea. It is at the end of summer. It lasts three days. People always go home for the festival. They spend time with their families. They want to celebrate and give thanks for the food from the harvest.

Why do people all around the world celebrate the harvest?

Words in Context

Find these words in the reading. What do you think they mean?

weave **cloth** **contest** **festival** **harvest** **ancestors**

Everyone has a big feast on *Chuseok*. There are many kinds of food. People make special rice cakes called *songpyeon*.

Songpyeon (*song-pyahn*) usually have something sweet inside.

Some people buy new clothes to wear on *Chuseok*. There are dances and games.

Korean circle dance

Chuseok is also a time for Koreans to remember their ancestors. Families have a special ceremony. They bow and offer food from the harvest. This shows they care about their family. *Chuseok* is all about being thankful.

Is there a holiday like *Chuseok* in your country?

Explore the Reading

A Read and answer. How do people celebrate *Chuseok*?

B Read and complete. *Chuseok* is about being thankful. What are Korean people thankful for?

1 They are thankful for ______________________________ .

2 They are also thankful for ______________________________ .

C Think and discuss. What holidays or traditions do you have to show thanks?

My family has a big meal together to show thanks.

A Look and complete. How does each place make the character act and feel?

	Setting	Clara is ...	Clara feels ...
1			scared
2		laughing	
3			

~~scared~~ happy sad

~~laughing~~ climbing crying

The **setting** is the time and place in the story. One story can have many different settings.

B Look and complete. Compare and contrast the settings.

fruit ~~vegetables~~ family outside plants inside bowls

In the Kitchen

Both

vegetables

On the Farm

C Think and discuss. When is the harvest in your country? What foods are ready? How do people celebrate?

Our harvest is in the fall. Apples, corn, and potatoes are ready.

Now read **First Harvest**

Fiction

First Harvest

Harvest time is here. The family works hard on the farm. They dig up vegetables. They pick fruit.

"I'm worried. It's hard for plants to grow here. There isn't much water," says Dad.

What do you think the setting is?

"I don't believe it! These carrots are beautiful," says Dad.

Why is the family so happy about the harvest?

There are pink potatoes and purple corn. There are tomatoes with red and green stripes. There is a red pineapple. There are orange peas.

"We have a lot of food!" says August.

"And we worked hard for it," says Dad. "Thank you!"

Words in Context

Find these words in the reading. What do you think they mean?

pick **worried** **grow** **believe** **stripes**

“How can we celebrate?” asks Mom.
“I know, let’s get everyone together. We can have a feast!” says Ruth.

"That's a great idea," says Dad. "This is our very first harvest, after all."

"I want to make an apple pie," says Mom. "You two can help."

"Can we go outside and play first?" asks Ruth. "Please?"

"Oh, all right," says Dad.

"Check your space suits before you go," Mom says. "And make sure you have a lot of air."

"We will!" say August and Ruth.

A **space suit** is the clothing astronauts wear in space.

Explore the Reading

A **Look and read. Answer the questions.**

1 Where does the family grow their food?

They grow it on the farm.

2 What is one vegetable the family grows?

3 What is the setting of the story?

4 Who goes outside to play?

5 What does Mom ask the children to check?

B **Think, write, and discuss. Why is it hard to grow food on Mars?**

There are a lot of rocks.

C **Imagine you live on Mars. What's different? How does it make you feel? Draw the setting. Draw yourself.**

Phonics –*st*

Listen and say.

fast   last   lost   best   test

Now find more words ending with –*st* in the reading.

Why do we celebrate harvests?

A Think and write. Compare and contrast the two harvest stories in this unit.

What's the Same?	What's Different?
They both have families.	

B Think and discuss. Imagine you are a farmer. Make a table about your harvest and your celebration. Do a Think, Pair, Share.

Our harvest has ...
Our celebration has ...

For our harvest, we pick apples. For our celebration, we dance.

My Reading Journal

Be the author. Choose *Chuseok: Korea's Harvest Festival* or *First Harvest*. Read the ending again. Write and draw what happens next.

Do you like this unit? How many golden apples do you give it? Circle.

UNIT 3

It Keeps Changing

See, Think, Wonder

A Look at the picture. What do you see?

I see a lot of pink.

There are so many rocks!

B What do you think?

There's paint in the water.

I don't think he's safe.

C What do you wonder?

Is it juice?

What is he doing?

D Think and discuss. What good and bad changes in nature do you know about?

E Think and discuss. Look at this picture. Compare and contrast this setting to where you live.

Now read **The Bear and I**

Fiction

The Bear and I

I'm from a land of wind and cold,
With fields of ice and snow.
My story starts when I was young,
Many years ago.

How many **stanzas** does this poem have?

My fishing hole was in the ice,
Each morning, fish were there.
But one day I was face to face,
With a giant arctic bear.

What are the dangers for the man in the poem?

Words in Context

Find these words in the reading. What do you think they mean?

hole **twice** **enemy** **thin** **trap** **melting**

After many warm winters,
The ice on the sea was thin.
One morning, the bear was near me,
Crack! The bear and I fell in.

It was difficult to swim
In a trap of ice and sea.
But we were in the trap together,
The bear was not my enemy.

Why do you think the ice was a trap?

From that day on, it was clear,
Things change as years go by.
There is danger in this changing world,
For the bear and I.

Today the ice is melting,
And I am getting old,
But I hope to see the bear once more,
Living in the cold.

Does the man change his mind about the bear?

Explore the Reading

A **Read and write *True* or *False*.**

1 When the man was young, the bear was his friend. False

2 The man was hungry. ______

3 The ice was thin because the winters were cold. ______

4 Some of the changes are bad for the man and the bear. ______

5 At the end of the poem, the man doesn't want to see the bear. ______

B **Read and answer. Then write the number of the stanza where you can find the answer.**

Question	Answer	Stanza
1 Where is the man from?	a land of wind and cold	1
2 How big is the polar bear?		
3 Why is the ice thin?		
4 Why are they in the water?		
5 What does the man hope?		

C **Think and discuss. Do you think the man and the bear are friends at the end of the poem? Why or why not?**

I think they're not friends because the bear takes his fish.

Phonics –*ng*

Listen and say.

sing long reading bang spring

Now find more words ending with –*ng* in the reading.

A Read and check (✓) the answers. Compare and contrast the bear and the man from the poem.

- ✓ eats fish ✓
- is big and scary
- lives in the Arctic
- is hungry
- falls in the water
- lives in a house

Compare means find the similarities, or things that are the same.
Contrast means find the differences, or things that aren´t the same.

B Look and read. Circle things that are the same. Draw a line under things that are different. Compare with a partner.

1 It's red and has four wheels. It's big, noisy, and fast.

2 This car is small, fast, and quiet. It's white and has four wheels.

C Think, write, and discuss. What do we use cars for?

Now read **Clean Cars**

Nonfiction

Clean Cars

Cars are everywhere! We use them to go shopping, go to school, and go on vacation.

What are good and bad things about cars?

A lot of cars use gasoline for energy. Gasoline comes from oil in the ground. Gasoline cars are fast, but they are noisy and make the air dirty. Dirty air is bad for animals, plants, and people. It changes our climate, too.

gasoline | petrol

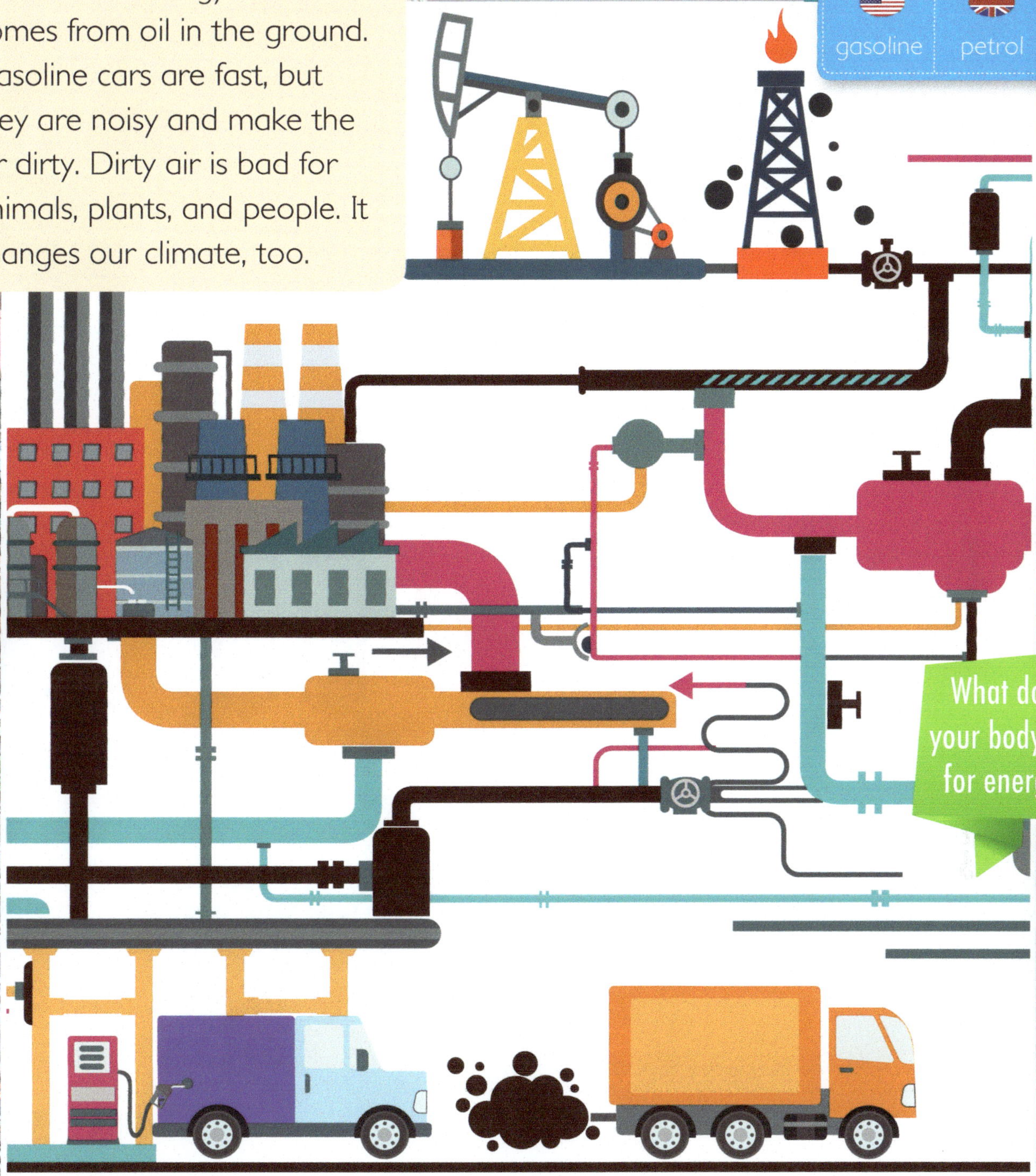

What does your body use for energy?

Words in Context

Find these words in the reading. What do you think they mean?

gasoline **energy** **oil** **noisy** **electricity** **expensive**

Not long ago, most cars were gasoline cars. Now some cars use biofuels. Biofuels come from plants like corn, but these plants need big fields and a lot of water. These cars make the air only a little dirty. Like gasoline cars, they go fast, but they aren't very quiet. They are very noisy.

Today, there are clean cars that don't use gasoline or biofuel. These cars use electricity, just like a TV or a lamp. They are fast and quiet. They are clean, but they are expensive.

Electric cars aren't new. The first car to go 100 km. per hour was an electric car in 1899.

Other cars use air for energy. They are not very expensive. They are quiet and clean, but they are small and slow.

Solar cars use energy from the sun. Some of them are fast. There are even races! They are not noisy or dirty, but they can be expensive. Not many people have them.

Do you like cars? Why or why not?

Clean cars are one way to have a clean world.

Explore the Reading

A Look and read. Find words in the reading and label the cars.

1  a ______________ car

3  a ______________ car

2  an ______________ car

4  a ______________ car

B Read and complete the table using these words. Use some words more than once.

fast **slow** **noisy** **quiet** **dirty** **clean** **small** **expensive**

Type of car	Good things	Bad things
gasoline	fast	
biofuel		
electric		
air		
solar		

C What's the main idea of the article? Read and check (✔).

1 Some cars are noisy and other cars are quiet. ◯

2 Clean cars are good for the world. ◯

3 We need cars to go to different places. ◯

D Think and discuss. Which clean car is your favorite? Why?

I like the solar car because it's fast and quiet.

How can we make good changes in our world?

A Think and write. What problems does climate change make for people and animals?

Climate Change

People

___

___

___

Animals

___

___

___

B Think and discuss. What changes can you make to keep our world clean? Do a Numbered Heads Together routine.

I can clean up trash because trash is a danger for animals.

I can ride a bike to school because bikes don't make the air dirty.

My Reading Journal

Now I know some new things about:

polar bears	yes / no	clean cars	yes / no
life in the Arctic	yes / no	climate change	yes / no

How does this unit make you feel? Write and draw how you feel.

I feel ___

___

___.

UNIT 4

What Happened?

Think, Pair, Share

A Look at the picture. Why is it in the park? Where is it now? Think about it.

B Talk with your partner.

What do you think?

I think it's in the park for decoration. What about you?

C Share with the class.

We think it's a new decoration.

D Think and discuss. What famous events in history do you know?

E Think and discuss. Look at the museum at the beginning and end of the story. What changes can you see?

Now read **Where Is She?**

Nonfiction

Where Is She?

In 1503, Leonardo da Vinci painted the *Mona Lisa*.

In 1911, Vincenzo Peruggia walked into the Louvre Museum in Paris. Peruggia had a plan. He wanted to steal the painting.

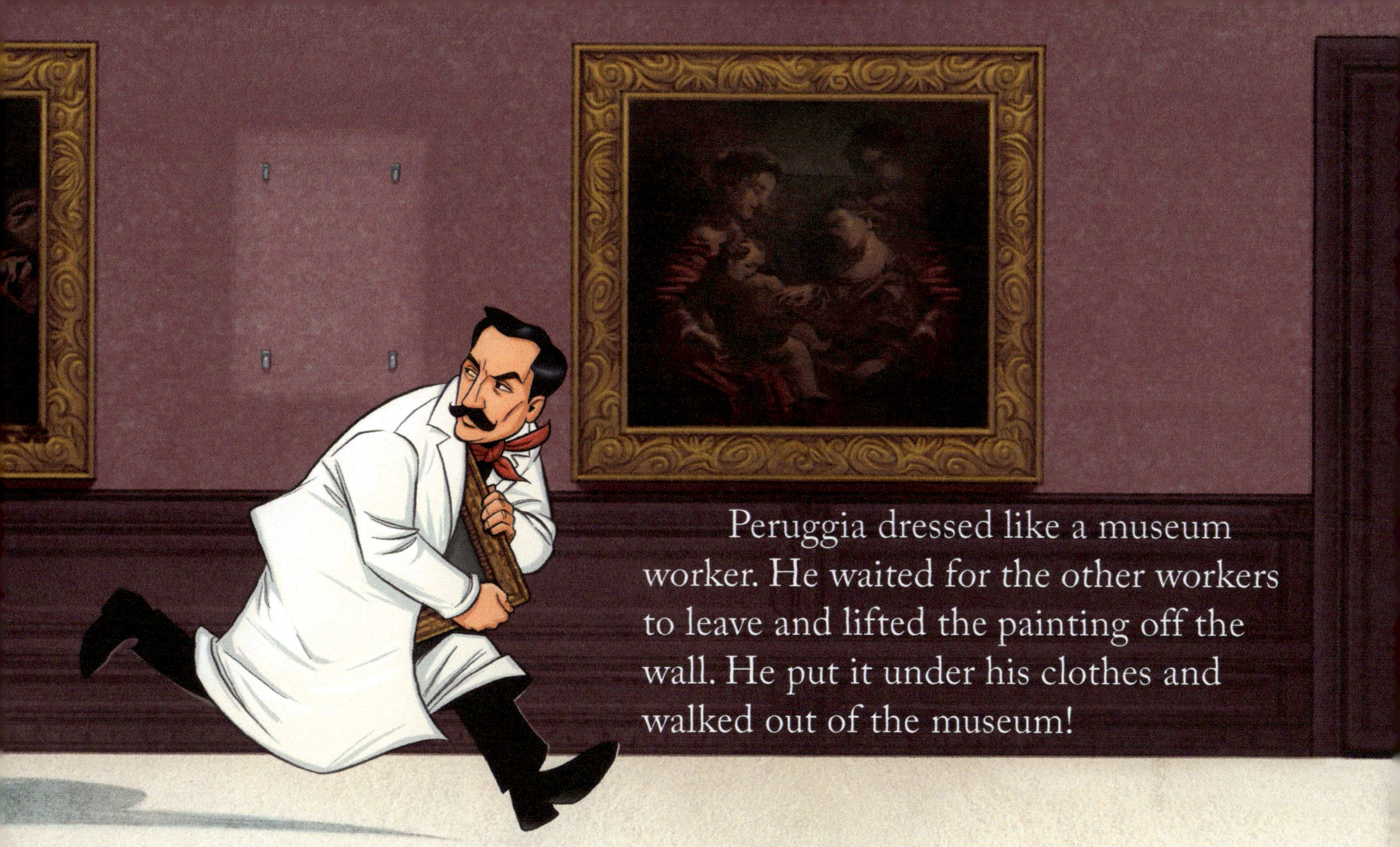

Peruggia dressed like a museum worker. He waited for the other workers to leave and lifted the painting off the wall. He put it under his clothes and walked out of the museum!

On the way out, he took the painting out of the frame. He rolled it up and hid it again. He walked out the door.

Words in Context

Find these words in the reading. What do you think they mean?

plan | steal | lifted | robbery | arrested

The next day, someone wanted to see the *Mona Lisa*. But there was only an empty space on the wall. A museum worker called the police.

Soon, the *Mona Lisa* was in the news all over the world. Everyone learned about the robbery.

People lined up to see the empty space on the wall! The *Mona Lisa* was famous.

lined up
queued

For two years, the police couldn't find the painting. Where was the *Mona Lisa*?

In 1913, Peruggia tried to sell the *Mona Lisa*.

The man looked at the painting and then called the police.

They arrested Peruggia.

At last, the *Mona Lisa* returned home to the Louvre. Because of the robbery, the *Mona Lisa* is one of the most famous paintings in the world!

Explore the Reading

A **Read and choose the answer.**

1 What did Vincenzo Peruggia want to do?

a. go to art class b. steal a painting c. be a museum guard

2 Where did Peruggia put the *Mona Lisa*?

a. in his hat b. under his clothes c. on the wall

3 What did people line up to see?

a. the news b. the key c. the empty space

4 How many years did it take for the police to find the painting?

a. two b. twenty c. twelve

5 Who did the police arrest?

a. Mona Lisa b. Peruggia c. the art dealer

B **Think and discuss. Do you think someone can steal a painting from a museum today? Why or why not?**

Yes, but a very small one.

No, there are alarms!

C **Imagine you work at a newspaper. The *Mona Lisa* is missing. Draw the museum worker's face when the painting is missing and when it is found.**

Missing

Found

A Look at the pictures. Match what happened and why.

1 

Clara's room is a mess.

2 

They dig up vegetables and pick fruit.

3 

The ice on the sea was thin.

a They have a feast.

b She invents a clean-up machine.

c They fall in the water.

A **cause** is why something happens. The cause is the reason. The **effect** is what happens. The effect is what changes.

B Look at these pictures. Write *Cause* or *Effect*.

1 

____

2 

____

C Think and draw. Are you scared sometimes? What makes you scared? Draw the cause and the effect.

Cause	Effect

Now read **The Angry Mountain**

Fiction

The Angry Mountain

That evening, I played on the beach by Papa's boat. Then the loud noises started. It sounded like thunder. Under my feet, the ground moved. Then it stopped. It was the mountain. Mount Tambora was angry again.

I wanted to see more, so I climbed a tree. I looked out at Mount Tambora. Fire went up into the sky. There was fire everywhere.

How did people's lives change?

I needed to find Mama and Papa.

The village streets were full of people. Dogs barked, people shouted. No one knew what to do. Some people went inside and locked their doors. A big cloud filled the sky.

Some mountains are volcanoes, like Mount Tambora.

Words in Context

Find these words in the reading. What do you think they mean?

thunder — bark — ash — dream — sunrise

"We must leave," said Mama. Papa packed up our things. We carried our things and ran to our boat. Ash and stones fell down from the sky. It was so dark. We couldn't see the mountain anymore.

In 1815, the explosion of Mount Tambora in Indonesia was the largest in history.

The small boat bounced up and down over large waves. More sounds of thunder came from the mountain. Mama hugged me close. I tried to sleep, but my dreams were full of scary things.

The next morning, at sunrise, we looked back at the island, and I cried. Nothing was left of our home—just ash and stones.

Why do you think the girl has bad dreams?

Then we saw a ship on the sea. We waved and it saw us. We were finally safe. Our home was gone, but we had each other.

Explore the Reading

A Read and answer.

1 What is the name of the mountain in the story?

The mountain's name is Mount Tambora.

2 Where is the girl playing?

3 Why does the girl climb the tree?

4 What fell down from the sky?

5 How do they leave the island?

B Think and discuss. Why do you think some people went inside and locked their doors?

Because they wanted to hide.

C Think, choose, and write. Imagine you lived near Mount Tambora in 1815. How do you feel?

sad hot happy safe bored scared bad angry thankful strong

I feel ______.

Phonics –*nd*

Listen and say.

end stand wind send find hand

Now find more words ending with –*nd* in the reading.

How do events change our lives?

A Read and complete. Both readings have causes and effects. Complete the table.

Cause	Effect
1 Peruggia steals the *Mona Lisa*.	
2	The man calls the police. The police arrest Peruggia.
3 The girl wants to see more.	
4	It is so dark, the family can't see the mountain anymore.

B Think and discuss. What were some important events in your life? Do a Three-Step Interview.

What was an important event for you?

My family moved to a new town last year.

Mia moved to a new town last year.

My Reading Journal

Choose your favorite character from *The Angry Mountain* or *Where Is She?* Think of three questions you want to ask him or her.

1 ______

2 ______

3 ______

Think of someone who would like this unit. Why did you choose him or her?

I choose ______ because ______.

UNIT 5

Let's Go Back

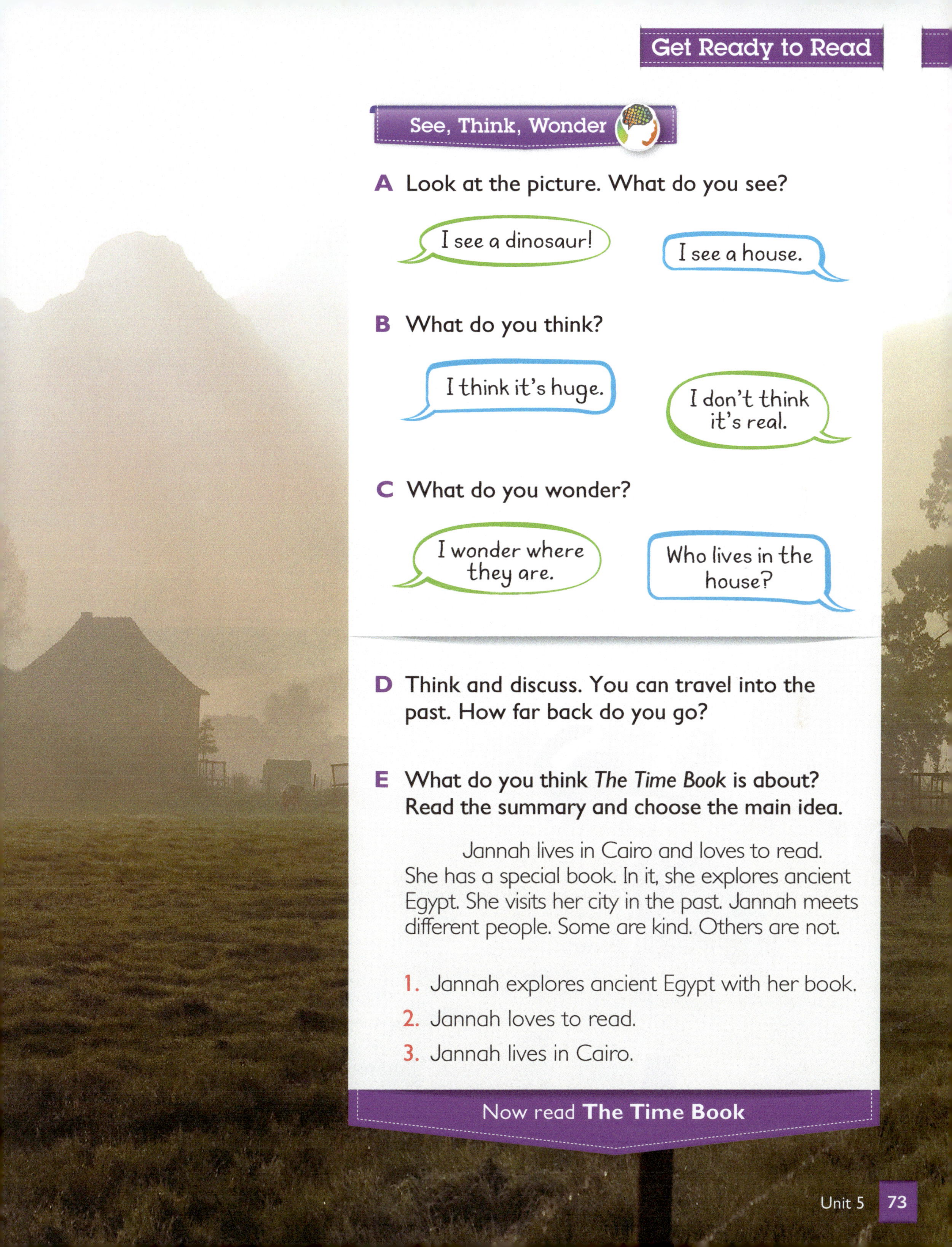

See, Think, Wonder

A Look at the picture. What do you see?

I see a dinosaur!

I see a house.

B What do you think?

I think it's huge.

I don't think it's real.

C What do you wonder?

I wonder where they are.

Who lives in the house?

D Think and discuss. You can travel into the past. How far back do you go?

E What do you think *The Time Book* is about? Read the summary and choose the main idea.

Jannah lives in Cairo and loves to read. She has a special book. In it, she explores ancient Egypt. She visits her city in the past. Jannah meets different people. Some are kind. Others are not.

1. Jannah explores ancient Egypt with her book.
2. Jannah loves to read.
3. Jannah lives in Cairo.

Now read **The Time Book**

The Time Book

It was time for Jannah to go to bed. *Just one more story*, she thought. *What's this? I don't remember this book. It looks interesting.*

On the book, there was a picture of an old street with a lot of people. She saw a girl. *That girl looks like me!* she thought. *How strange!*

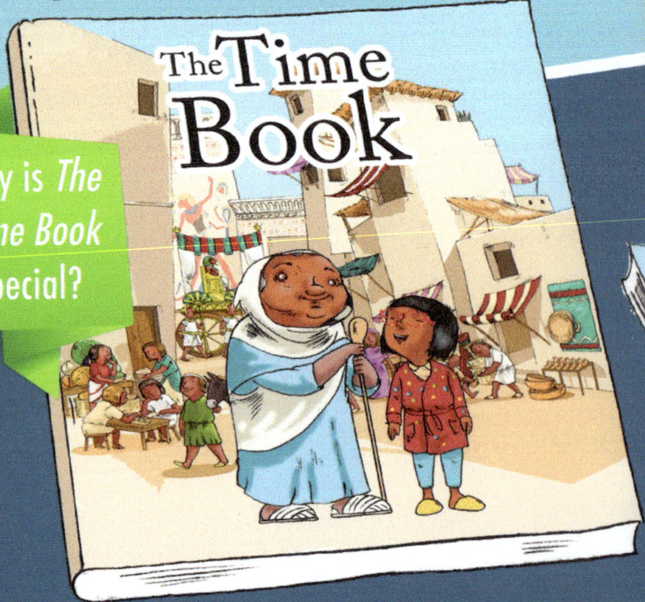

Why is *The Time Book* special?

She opened the book.

"Oh! Where am I?" asked Jannah. She was in a very old city.

"Look!" said an old woman next to her. "The pharaoh is coming."

Words in Context

Find these words in the reading. What do you think they mean?

strange pharaoh chariot surprised scared ancient

"I want to see the pharaoh," said the woman. Then Jannah saw the huge chariot. "Look out!" she shouted.

"Oh, thank you," said the woman. "I can't see very well."

"Try my glasses," said Jannah.

"Glasses?"

"Yes, they help you see. Put them in front of your eyes."

The old woman was surprised. "Now I can see everything. There's the pharaoh!"

The ancient Egyptians made glass, but they didn't have eyeglasses yet.

“Who’s that girl?” asked the pharaoh. “What strange clothes. Stop her!”

“Oh, no! They’re coming,” said the old woman. “Run!” Jannah was scared. *Did I do something wrong?* she thought. She turned and ran.

“Wait!” shouted a guard.

Jannah ran through the ancient city. The streets were hot and dark. Suddenly, there was a hand on her shoulder.

“Wake up, Jannah,” said her mom.

Jannah sat up in bed. She looked at the book. “That’s strange,” she said. “The picture looks different.”

“... And where are my glasses?”

Explore the Reading

A **Read and write *True* or *False*.**

1 Jannah lived in ancient Egypt. False

2 She liked reading. ______

3 The old woman didn't like Jannah. ______

4 The old woman helped Jannah. ______

5 Jannah woke up in the old woman's house. ______

B **Read and answer the questions.**

1 Where is Jannah when the story starts and ends?

Jannah is in bed when the story starts and ends.

2 Why did Jannah look different to the people in ancient Egypt?

______

3 Why did Jannah run?

______

4 Whose hand was on Jannah's shoulder?

______

5 What was strange about the book cover at the end of the story?

______

C **Think and discuss. Which of these things did ancient Egyptians <u>not</u> have? How did that make their lives different from yours?**

chariot, writing, cats, paper, horses, fruit, glasses, bread

A **Read the paragraph. What's the main idea? Underline the answer.**

Jannah lived in Cairo. With her special book, she explored Cairo in ancient Egypt. She saw many things that were different than in her city. She met people from the past.

The **main idea** gives the most important information. It's the big idea! The **details** give extra information so you understand more.

B **Read the paragraph. Then write** *Main Idea* **or** *Detail* **for each sentence.**

[1]Many different things can go inside a time capsule. [2]People put letters, pictures, and objects in them. [3]They put them in the ground. [4]In the future, other people can dig and find them.

1 __________

2 __________

3 __________

4 __________

C **Think and discuss. Name things you want to put in a time capsule.**

I want to put in my favorite video game.

In my time capsule, there's a photo of my city.

Now read **Time Capsules**

Nonfiction

Time Capsules

Do you want people in the future to know about your life right now? One way you can do this is to make a time capsule. It's like giving a present from the past.

Many different things can go inside a time capsule. People put letters, pictures, and objects in them. Kids put cool things like movies, music, video games, and toys in time capsules. They put them in the ground. In the future, other people can dig and find them.

What is a time capsule?

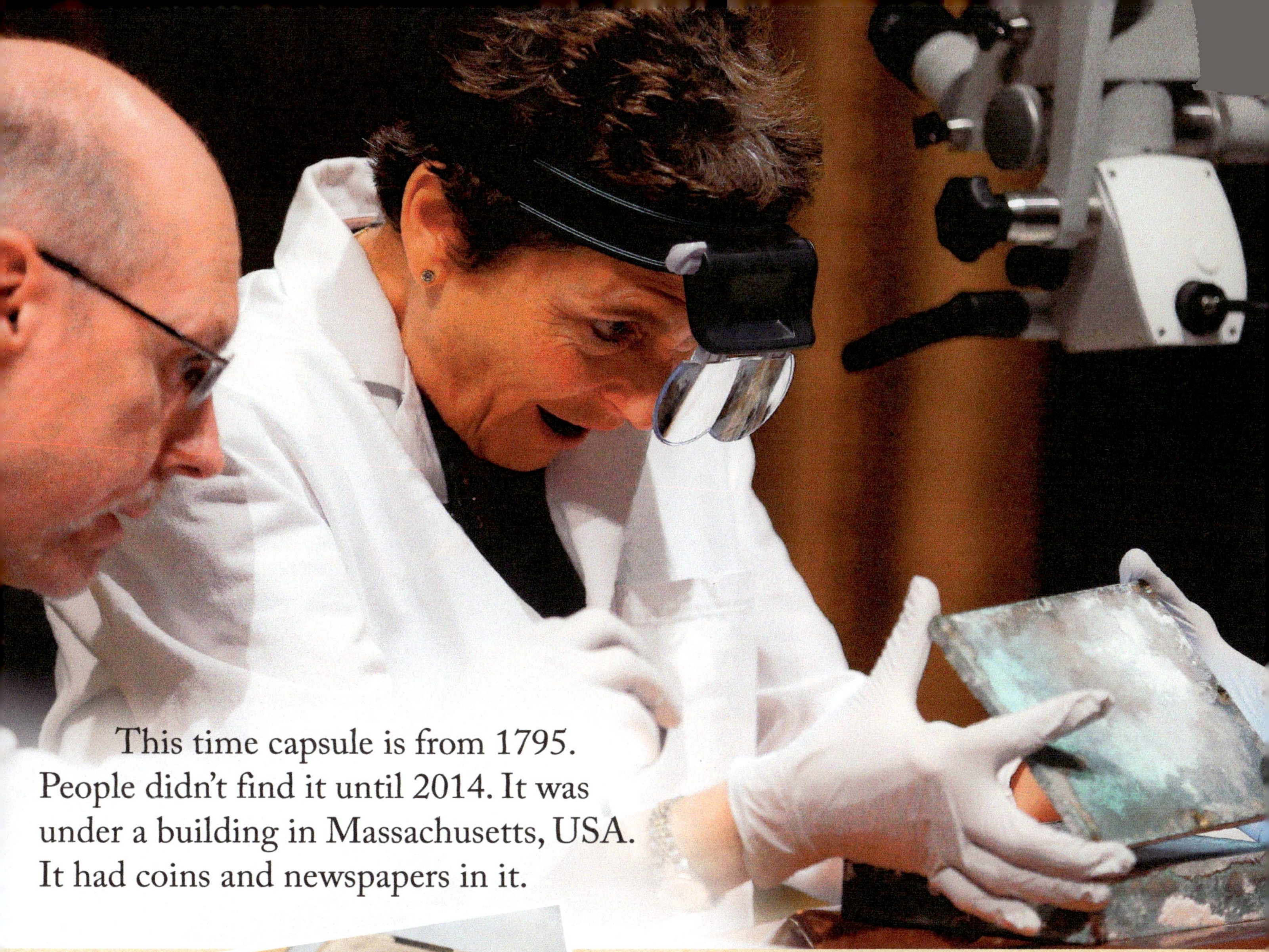

This time capsule is from 1795. People didn't find it until 2014. It was under a building in Massachusetts, USA. It had coins and newspapers in it.

How many years did it take to find the time capsule?

Words in Context

Find these words in the reading. What do you think they mean?

future · objects · newspapers · spacecraft · disc · Earth

More than forty years ago, people put time capsules in two spacecraft called *Voyager 1* and *Voyager 2*.

There are no people on the spacecraft, but each one has a gold disc. The gold disc is a time capsule. It says *hello* in 55 different languages.

How many languages can you say *hello* in?

On the disc, there are also sounds of the sea, wind, thunder, and rain. There are the songs of birds, whales, and people. It also has photos of people, animals, and places on Earth.

Voyager 1 and *Voyager 2* went into space in 1977. Now, they are billions of kilometers from Earth. They are still in space today.

These are real photographs on the gold disc. Do they look old or new?

Explore the Reading

A Read and choose the answer.

1 People leave things in time capsules for people in the past / future to find.

2 The time capsule from 1795 had coins and pictures / newspapers in it.

3 People put time capsules on the *Voyager* spacecraft over forty / ninety years ago.

4 On the gold disc there are messages in one language / a lot of languages.

5 The *Voyager* spacecraft are on Earth / in space now.

B Read and think. Then match. What's the main idea of each page?

1 page 82	a. time capsules from the past
2 page 83	b. time capsules in spacecraft
3 page 84	c. what's inside the spacecraft's time capsule
4 page 85	d. what a time capsule is

C Check (✔) two things to tell people in the future about. Write a message.

- ◯ animals
- ◯ things you do every day
- ◯ transportation
- ◯ books and movies
- ◯ your school

My message

Phonics –nt

Listen and say.

point plant front invent student

Now find more words ending with –*nt* in the reading.

How can we find out about the past?

A Read, think, and check (✔).

Someone ...	*The Time Book*	*Time Capsules*
1 looks at pictures in a book	✔	
2 looks at coins and newspapers		
3 reads a story about the past		
4 finds something old in the ground		
5 imagines life in an ancient city		
6 writes messages for the future		

B **Take the quiz. What do you do to learn about the past?**

1 Do you read nonfiction books? yes / no

2 Do you talk to your family? yes / no

3 Do you dig for fossils? yes / no

4 Do you watch movies with settings in the past? yes / no

5 Do you look at old pictures of your town? yes / no

6 Do you go to museums? yes / no

C **Think and discuss. Share your ideas for learning about the past. Do an Inside-Outside Circle.**

My Reading Journal

Find five words that are interesting or new to you. Write.

1 ______ 2 ______ 3 ______ 4 ______ 5 ______

What person or event from history do you want to find out about?

I want to learn about ______________________________

______________________________.

UNIT 6

Look What I Made

Think, Pair, Share

A Look at the picture. Is this art? Think about it.

B Talk with your partner.

> What do you think?

> I think it is because someone made it. What about you?

C Share with the class.

> We think it *is* art!

D Think and discuss. Do you make or create things? What are they?

> I make jewelry with beads.

E Read and choose. Which of these sentences is <u>not</u> true?

1. An artist needs tools to make a sculpture.
2. Sculptures can be outside or inside.
3. The best sculptures are of people.

Now read **The Superstar**

Fiction

Why do sculptors make statues of people?

"Hi, can I help you?" asked Pablo.

"Hi, I'm Whitney. Mr. Mateo Martinez, you know, the superstar, I'm his assistant. Can I see the sculpture, please?" asked Whitney. "Remember, it has to be finished before the celebration on Friday." Her phone rang.

"Excuse me," she said and answered it.

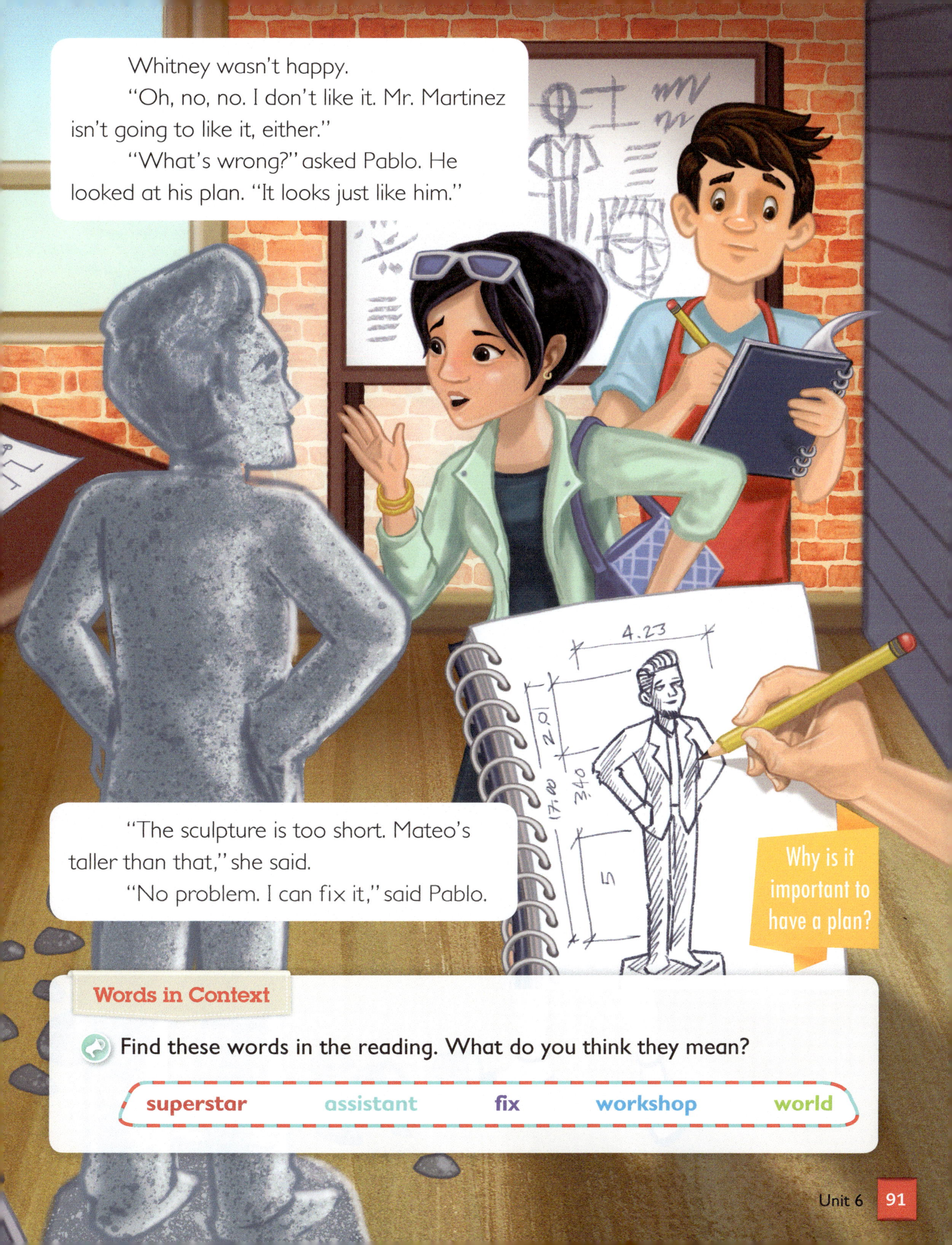

Whitney wasn't happy.

"Oh, no, no. I don't like it. Mr. Martinez isn't going to like it, either."

"What's wrong?" asked Pablo. He looked at his plan. "It looks just like him."

"The sculpture is too short. Mateo's taller than that," she said.

"No problem. I can fix it," said Pablo.

Why is it important to have a plan?

Words in Context

Find these words in the reading. What do you think they mean?

superstar **assistant** **fix** **workshop** **world**

The next day, Mateo's brother came to see the sculpture.

"It's not bad," he said. "But my brother's beard is longer and curlier."

"Don't worry. I can fix it," said Pablo.

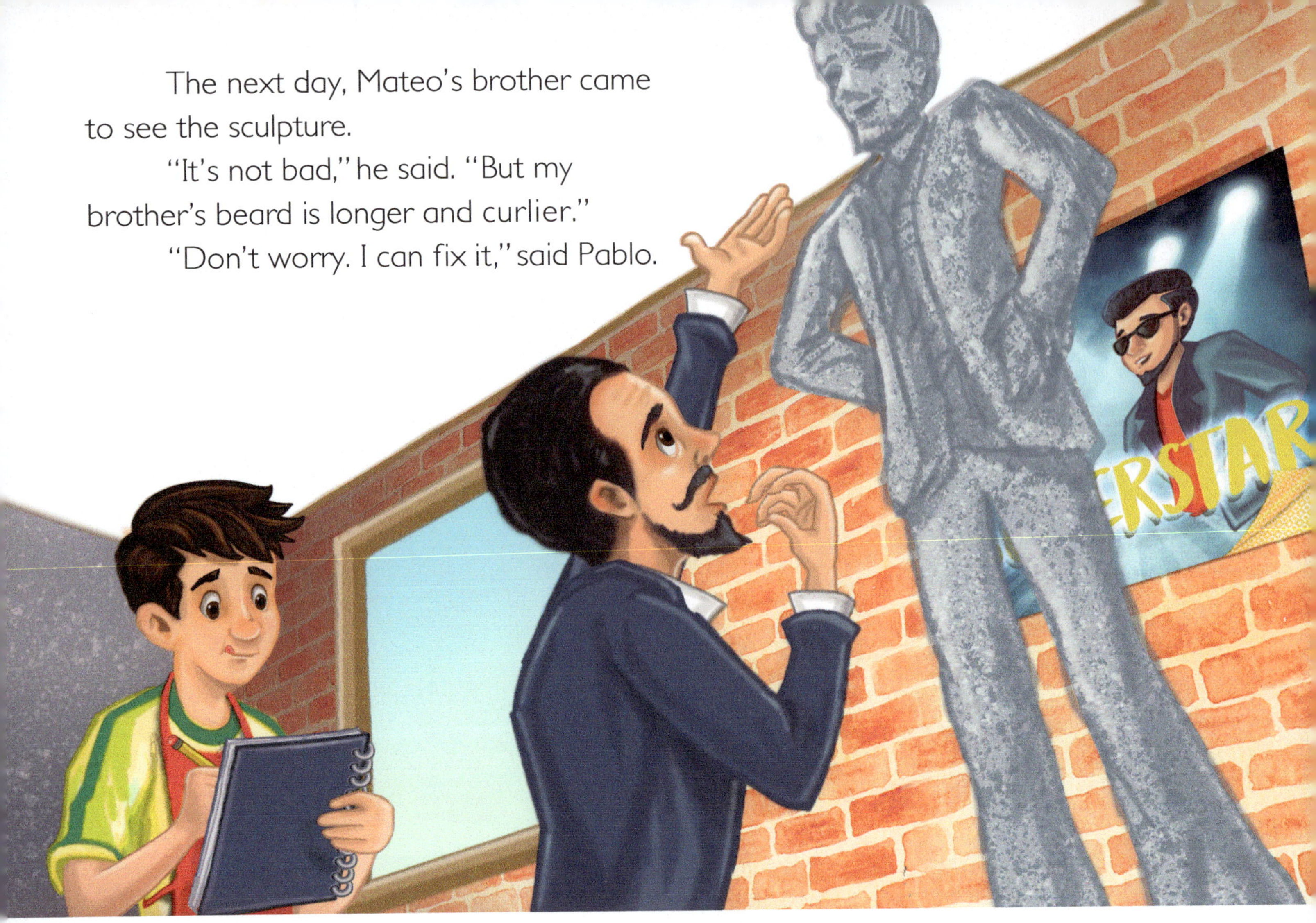

Later, Mateo's mother came to the workshop.

"My son's arms and hands need to be bigger," she said.

"Bigger?" asked Pablo.

"Much bigger," she said.

All week, it was noisy in Pablo's workshop.

Finally, he finished the sculpture.

Mateo came to see the sculpture.
"Thank you," he said.
"I travel all over the world for my movies, but I always love coming home!"

"Who is *that*?" asked Mateo.

"It's you," said Pablo.

"But it doesn't look like me! My beard is too long, I'm too tall, and my hands are huge! Please fix it!"

"Whoops! OK, but we need a new plan," said Pablo, "... or maybe the old one."

What famous sculptures do you know?

Explore the Reading

A Read and number. Put the sentences in order.

- [ ] All week, it was noisy in Pablo's workshop.
- [ ] Whitney wasn't happy. "Oh, no, no. I don't like it."
- [ ] Later, Mateo's mother came to the workshop.
- [ ] Finally, he finished the sculpture.
- [ ] "Can I see the sculpture please?" asked Whitney.

B Think and write. What changes did each person ask Pablo to make?

1  → ____________________

2  → ____________________

3  → ____________________

C Think and discuss. Did Pablo's plan help him? Why or why not? Do plans help you?

> Yes, it did. He knew what to do.

Phonics *wh–*

Listen and say.

whale wheel where whisper why

Now find more words starting with *wh–* in the reading.

A **Read and check (✔) the true sentences.**

1 The *Mona Lisa* is a famous painting by Leonardo da Vinci. ✔
2 The *Mona Lisa* is the best painting in the whole world.
3 Someone stole the painting from the Louvre Museum in 1911.
4 The Louvre is everyone's favorite museum.
5 The thief, Vincenzo Peruggia, had a nice mustache.

A **fact** is a piece of information that is correct and true.
An **opinion** is what someone thinks or believes.

B **Read and underline the opinions.**

1 Barcelona has some of the world's greatest buildings.
2 Antoni Gaudí died in 1926.
3 Antoni Gaudí designed beautiful buildings.
4 Park Güell is a wonderful park.
5 Casa Milà is an ugly building.

C **Think and discuss. When people create, where do they get their ideas? When you create, where do you get your ideas?**

Sometimes people go to the beach and paint what they see.

I get ideas for my drawings from stories.

Now read **Visit Gaudí's World**

Nonfiction

Visit Gaudí's World

The city of Barcelona in Spain has some of the world's greatest buildings. They look like they are from a children's storybook. They are the work of the famous architect Antoni Gaudí (1852–1926). Gaudí designed buildings and studied nature for ideas.

Why do Gaudí's buildings look so different?

In 1904, a man named Josep Batlló asked Gaudí to make him a new home. Gaudí's plan was to use round shapes and the colors of nature.

The front of the building looks like bones. The colors Gaudí used are the colors of coral from the sea. The walls look like flowers on water.

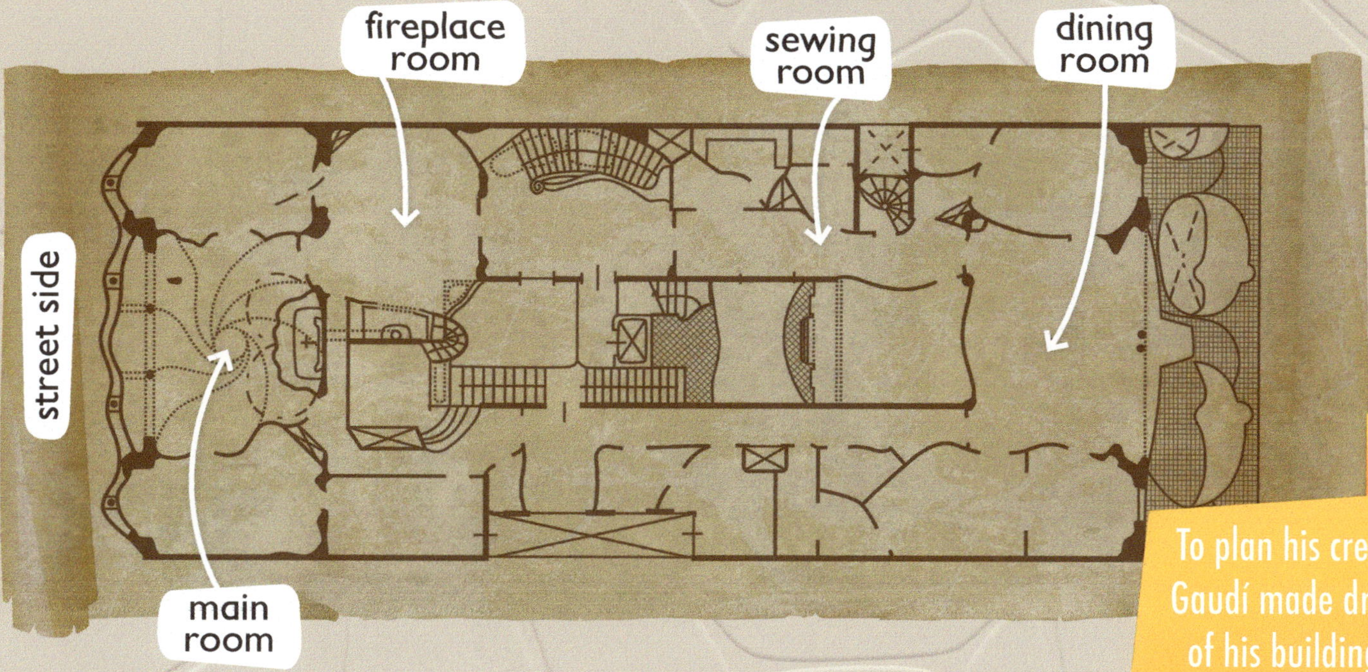

To plan his creations, Gaudí made drawings of his buildings. Do you like to draw?

Words in Context

Find these words in the reading. What do you think they mean?

architect nature coral bench cave

Gaudí also wanted to create somewhere for people to enjoy nature. In Park Güell, there is a famous sculpture in the shape of a lizard. There are stone walls that look like tree trunks. There is a bench in the shape of a sea snake.

Gaudí's buildings are UNESCO World Heritage sites! That means they're important for people to see.

Visit Casa Milà

Gaudí's plan for Casa Milà was for the building to look like nature, too. The front of the building looks like a stone quarry. Inside, part of the building looks a little like a cave. The building was home for the Milà family.

Join people from all over the world. Come and see the buildings of Antoni Gaudí.

Casa Milà's nickname is *The Quarry*. A quarry is a place where people dig out stones.

Explore the Reading

A **Read and check (✔). Which of these facts do we learn from the reading?**

1 Antoni Gaudí was a famous architect. ✔

2 Barcelona is Spain's second biggest city.

3 Gaudí was born in 1852.

4 Soccer is the most popular sport in Spain.

5 Some of Gaudí's famous works are Casa Milà, Park Güell, and Casa Batlló.

B **Look at the pictures. Where did Gaudí get his ideas from? Match the building to the idea.**

1

2

3

4

5

a

b

c
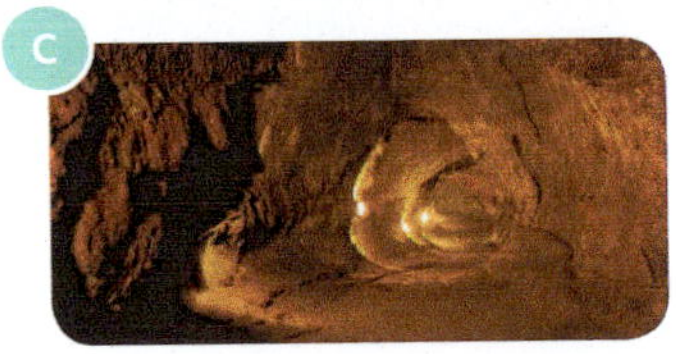

d

e

C **Think and discuss. Gaudí made his buildings look like nature. What do you want to make your buildings look like?**

I want my buildings to look like spaceships.

Why do people make things?

A Compare and contrast the creations. Fill in the table.

Creation	Reason	Type of Creation	Materials
Pablo's statue		sculpture	
Casa Milà			stone, glass, plaster
Park Güell		park	
Mona Lisa	a portrait for a home		

B Think and discuss. What other creations do you know in your country and around the world? Do a Round Robin.

In Dubai, there are statues of a man and woman.

C Think and discuss. Why do you think the people made those creations?

I think the statues are there because they make the city look nice.

My Reading Journal

Imagine you can visit one of the settings in this unit. Which one do you choose? Why?

I choose ______________________ because ______________________.

How much did you like this unit? Color the stars. ☆ ☆ ☆ ☆ ☆

UNIT 7

We're a Team

See, Think, Wonder

A Look at the picture. What do you see?

I see a lot of people.

There are many colors.

B What do you think?

I think they practiced a lot.

I think it is dangerous.

C What do you wonder?

Is it a holiday?

Does it hurt?

D Think and discuss. What things do you do in a team?

E Read and answer. What do you think happens at the end?

This man and this bird both like honey. They want to find some.

At the end, I think they ______________________________.

Now read **Great Teamwork**

Nonfiction

Great Teamwork

The Honey Hunters

The Boran people and the honey bird both live in Africa. Both like honey, but both have a problem. The Boran hunters don't know where the honey is. Honey birds know where to find the honey, but they can't get it out of the bees' nests.

The people and the honey birds help each other and work together. When a Boran hunter wants honey, he whistles and shouts. When a hungry honey bird is near, it answers with a special call.

There are two headings in this reading. Can you find them?

The bird flies through the forest and the hunter follows.

When they are near a bees' nest, the bird sings in a different way. This tells the hunter where the bees and honey are.

The hunter takes the honey from the nest, but he always leaves some for the bird to say *thank you*.

Honey birds also help other animals, like honey badgers, find honey. Can you find the badger?

Words in Context

Find these words in the reading. What do you think they mean?

hunters **both** **Africa** **whistles** **shrimp** **holds on** **entrance**

Good Friends

The gobie fish and the pistol shrimp are two very different animals, but they both need help. The gobie fish cannot dig, but the pistol shrimp can. The shrimp digs a hole in the sand where they both live.

The shrimp cannot see very well, but the fish can. When the shrimp is looking for food, it holds on to the fish. The fish watches for danger. It moves its tail to tell the shrimp that danger is near. The shrimp hides.

At night, the shrimp closes the entrance with sand. The fish and the shrimp sleep in the safe hole. They share their home.

Which example of teamwork is your favorite?

Explore the Reading

A **Read the questions. Check (✔) the correct answers.**

Who ...				
1 knows where the honey is?		✔		
2 takes the honey from the nest?				
3 eats the honey?				
4 digs but can't see very well?				
5 sees very well but can't dig?				
6 lives in the hole?				

B **Read and match.**

1 The hunter whistles and shouts
2 The honey bird sings in a different way
3 The hunter leaves some honey
4 The fish moves its tail
5 The shrimp closes the entrance to the hole

a. to tell the shrimp there is danger.
b. to tell the hunter he is near the honey.
c. to go to sleep in a safe place.
d. to call the honey bird.
e. to say *thank you* to the honey bird.

C **Read and answer. What makes a good team? Check (✔). Compare with a partner.**

1 sharing ideas ✔
2 listening to others
3 working alone
4 letting others do all the work
5 taking turns
6 helping each other
7 working together
8 being quiet

A Read the beginning and the middle of the story. Write an ending.

It is summer. Pablo is hot and hungry. He finds a gold coin in the grass. He puts it in his pocket.

He meets an old man. "I'm looking for my gold coin," says the man.

In my ending, ____

____

____.

Predicting the ending of a story helps us think about what might happen. We use what we know from the words and pictures to help us make good guesses.

B Think and discuss. Which ending do you like best? Why?

1 Pablo gives the old man the coin. "Thank you," says the old man. "Come to my house and share my food."

2 Pablo says nothing. He goes to a café for lunch. He puts his hand into his pocket, but the coin isn't there.

3 Pablo gives the coin back. "You're a good man," says the old man. He takes off his coat. "I'm from the TV show *Choices*. You did the right thing. Here is a prize for you."

Some stories have surprise endings. Do you know any?

C Read page 112. What do you think happens at the end of the reading?

I think they find treasure.

Now read **It's Mine!**

Fiction

It's Mine!

Close your book. Can you remember the password?

Words in Context

Find these words in the reading. What do you think they mean?

treasure password map grab rich gold pirate

Look, it's a map.
Give it to me!
Don't grab!
Oh, no!
Let's share the map.
Let's help each other.
Look! The treasure's there.
I saw it first!
Dig here
It's mine!

It's mine now.
Wait!
Teamwork!
I need help.
Let's take turns.
Good idea.
We're
rich!
No, I'm rich.
It's all mine.
The gold is mine.

Let's work together.
Quick! Put it into the boat.
It's very heavy.
Goodbye!
Come back!
Wait for me.
Watch out!

I can't swim!
Oh, no! The treasure!
Let's look for treasure on another island.
Good idea.
From eight o'clock 'til half past three We sail across the big blue sea
From four o'clock 'til half past ten
We sail across the sea again Yes, it's a pirate's life for me.

Explore the Reading

A **Read and number. Put the events in order. Retell the story.**

☐ They carried the treasure to the boat.
☐ They opened the box and found a map.
☐ They found a box with a note.
☐ They dug in the sand and found the treasure.
1 Three pirates arrived on an island.
☐ The treasure fell in the sea.

B **Read and choose.**

1 At the end of the story,

a. the pirates took the treasure and sailed away.

b. the pirates found the treasure and lived together on the island.

c. the pirates didn't work together and lost the treasure.

d. the pirates shared the treasure with the parrot.

2 The ending matches my prediction.

a. Yes

b. No

C **Think and discuss. Did the pirates work together? Were they a good team? Why or why not?**

> They sailed the boat together.

Phonics *–ck*

Listen and say.

sock black backpack neck duck

Now find more words ending in –*ck* in the reading.

What is good about teamwork?

A Read and write *Yes* or *No*. Then compare with a partner.

	The honey bird and the hunter	The shrimp and the fish	The three pirates
1 They are good at sharing.			
2 They take turns.			
3 They always help each other.			
4 They listen to others.			

B Think and discuss. Are these good teams? Why or why not? Do a Think, Pair, Share.

1

2

3

My Reading Journal

Pick a reading and change the ending. How does this change the story?

Color the coins to rate each reading in this unit.

Great Teamwork ① ① ① ① ①

It's Mine! ① ① ① ① ①

UNIT 8 You're My Hero

See, Think, Wonder

A Look at the picture. What do you see?

I see a boy on their shoulders.

There is a cat in the window.

B What do you think?

I think it's a party.

They're proud of the boy.

C What do you wonder?

Why are they holding him?

I wonder whose birthday it is?

D Think and discuss. What makes someone a hero?

E Look at the pictures in the reading. Who is the main character? Which adjectives do you think describe him? Think and check (✔).

- ◯ strong
- ◯ brave
- ◯ bored
- ◯ funny
- ◯ tall
- ◯ sad

Now read **In First Place**

Nonfiction

In *First* Place

In the Olympic Games, the marathon is a very long and difficult running race. It is 42 km. long. One of the most famous Olympic marathon runners was a man named Abebe Bikila.

Bikila was born in Ethiopia in 1932. He was the son of a shepherd. As a young man, he joined the army. In the army, he learned to run well and win races.

Every four years, the world's best athletes compete at the Olympic Games.

How do you think Bikila felt when he joined the Olympic team?

In 1960, Wami Biratu, one of the runners on the Ethiopian team, hurt his foot. He could not go to the Olympics. At the last minute, Bikila took his place.

The team had shoes for Biratu, but not Bikila. The shoes weren't comfortable and Bikila's feet hurt. He decided to run barefoot, so he was more comfortable.

Words in Context

Find these words in the reading. What do you think they mean?

Olympic Games **hurt** **comfortable** **barefoot** **medal**

At the start of the race, people didn't know his name. Some people wondered who he was. Some people laughed when they saw Bikila did not have shoes.

Why do you think some people laughed at Abebe Bikila?

It was a tough race, but Bikila was strong. After a while, there were only two runners in front of him. With 1 km. left in the race, Bikila pushed himself. Soon, the brave runner was in first place.

Bikila kept running. He crossed the finish line and won the gold medal! Then everyone knew his name. No one laughed at him.

In the 1964 Olympic Games, Bikila ran the marathon with shoes. He won the gold medal a second time.

Abebe Bikila is a great athlete and a hero for people around the world.

Abebe Bikila was the first person to win the Olympic marathon twice in a row.

Explore the Reading

A Read and write *True* or *False*.

1 The marathon is a short running race. False
2 Abebe Bikila ran his first Olympic marathon barefoot. ____
3 At the start of the race, Abebe Bikila was famous. ____
4 Abebe Bikila lost the race. ____
5 In 1964, Abebe Bikila ran the Olympic marathon wearing shoes. ____
6 Abebe Bikila won two gold medals. ____

B Put the events in order.

☐ People laughed at Abebe Bikila.
☐ It was a tough race but he pushed himself.
1 Bikila took the other runner's place.
☐ He crossed the finish line and won the gold medal!
☐ His shoes made his feet hurt.
☐ Soon, he was in first place.

C Think, write, and discuss. How do you think Abebe Bikila felt?

thankful sad brave scared surprised happy

1 Before the race, he felt ____ and ____.
2 At the race, he felt ____ and ____.
3 After the race, he felt ____ and ____.

D Think and discuss. What other famous people from history do you know?

I know Margarete. She made the first teddy bear!

A Look, think, and discuss. What kinds of characters are they? How can you describe them?

Abebe Bikila was a real person.

The pirates aren't kind.

Characters are the people in a play, story, or poem. Sometimes they are made up. Sometimes they are real people. Characters think and act in many different ways.

B Match the characters to the sentences.

1 
Allie Gator

2 
Helicopter Harri

3 
X-Ray Bob

4 
Otto Octopus

a I can fly.

b I have special glasses.

c I have sharp teeth.

d I have eight strong arms.

C Think and discuss. Does a hero need to be someone famous? Does a hero need to be a grown-up?

My grandma is a hero, and she isn't famous.

My little sister helped a baby bird. So I think a kid can be a hero.

Now read **A New Hero**

Fiction

A New Hero

Mayor

Assistant

Allie Gator

Helicopter Harri

Otto Octopus

X-Ray Bob

Narrator: Rockham City wants a new hero. They want someone to make the city a better place. The Mayor and her assistant meet people for the job.

Assistant: Hello, welcome to the Mayor's office.

Allie Gator: Hi, I'm Allie Gator.

Mayor: Hello, what do you do?

Allie Gator: I snap my teeth at robbers.

Who is the hero in this play?

Mayor: Very good. Next!

Words in Context

Find these words in the reading. What do you think they mean?

City Mayor job robber X-ray

Mayor: Wow!
Narrator: A young boy knocks on the door. He looks small and shy.
Assistant: Who are you?
Bob: My name is Bob.
Mayor: You're a kid. What makes you a hero?

Bob: On my way home from school, I pick up trash in the park.
Mayor: Hmm.
Bob: I help people carry their shopping bags, even though they can be heavy.
Mayor: I see …

trash
math

rubbish
maths

Bob: I always help my neighbor with his homework. In school, I find math really hard, but I try my best.
Mayor: But those are small things.

Bob: Little things add up. Oh, and I have these X-ray glasses. I can see through anything!

Allie Gator: I can't find my keys!
Bob: There they are.
Allie Gator: Thank you so much.
How do "little things" make a place better or worse?

Allie Gator: This kid's a true hero!
Helicopter Harri: Oh, yes!
Otto Octopus: He is the most helpful hero!
Mayor: You're right! X-Ray Bob is just the person this city needs. The job is yours!
Bob: I can start tomorrow.
Mayor and Assistant: Great!
Which of these heroes do you like best?

Bob: Just as soon as I finish my homework.

Explore the Reading

A Think and answer. What makes Bob a hero? Check (✔).

1 Bob helps people carry their shopping bags. ✔
2 Bob flies around saving cats in trees.
3 Bob finds Allie Gator's keys.
4 Bob snaps his jaws at robbers.
5 Bob helps his neighbor with his homework.
6 Bob picks up trash in the park.
7 Bob uses his eight arms to help people in trouble.

B Draw and write. Create another hero at the mayor's office. What does your hero do in the city?

Name:

My hero can:

My hero helps the city when:

C Think and discuss. Imagine you are the Mayor. Who do you want to be the hero of Rockham City? Why did you choose that hero?

I want Otto Octopus because he has so many arms.

Phonics *tr–*

Listen and say.

tractor train travel trip treasure

Now find more words starting with *tr–* in the reading.

What makes a hero?

A Think and write. Abebe Bikila and the heroes from *A New Hero* come to your class. What questions do you want to ask them?

This question is for …	I want to ask …
1	
2	
3	
4	

B Think and discuss. What are heroes like? What do they do? Do a Numbered Heads Together routine.

Heroes always try hard.

My Reading Journal

Imagine you are making a movie. Choose *In First Place* or *A New Hero*. Which do you choose? Why?

I choose ______________________________ because

____.

Abebe Bikila won the gold medal at the Olympics. Which medal do you give this unit? Circle one.

gold

silver

bronze

Why did you choose that medal?

____.

UNIT 9

Do You Live Here?

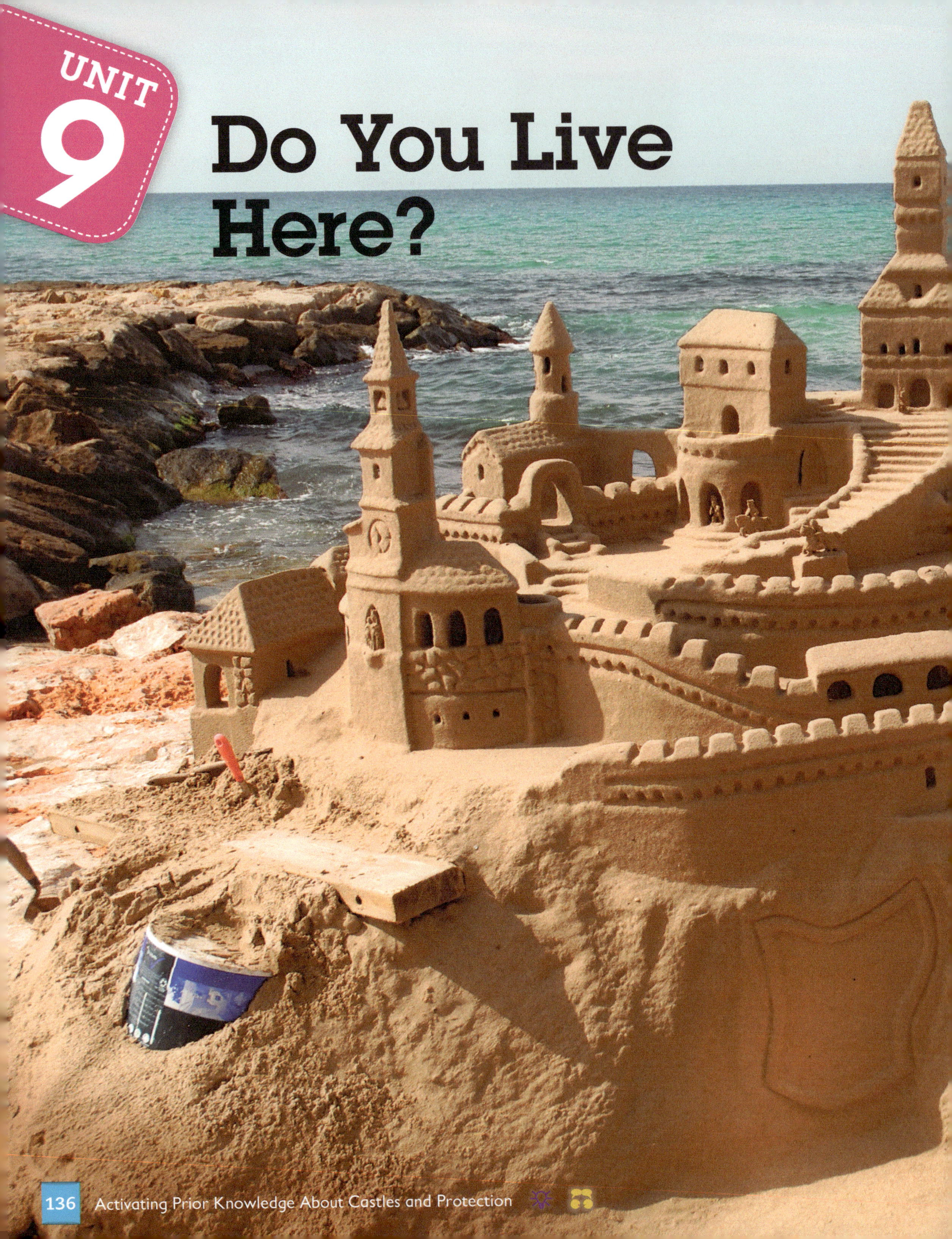

Think, Pair, Share

A Look at the picture. Does anyone live there? Think about it.

B Talk with your partner.

What do you think?

Maybe a crab lives there. What do you think?

C Share with the class.

We think it's a crab castle!

D Think, write, and discuss. What do you know about castles? What do you want to find out about them?

I Know ...	I Want to Find Out ...

E Read page 138 quickly. Answer these questions.

1 Where did the king live? ____________

2 What didn't he want? ____________

Now read **The Clever King**

Fiction

The Clever King

Once upon a time, there was a grumpy dragon king. He lived alone in an old castle, and he wasn't very friendly.

I don't want anybody in my castle, he thought. *Hmm, I have an idea.*

Why does the king make changes to his castle?

First, he made an automatic drawbridge. When dragons came near his castle, the bridge went up. ***Creak!*** The king was very pleased.

"Ha, ha!" he shouted from the window.

Listen to the word **castle** in the story. Can you hear the *t*?

"We don't want to come in," said the dragons, and they went away.

Words in Context

Find these words in the reading. What do you think they mean?

clever **grumpy** **automatic** **drawbridge** **moat** **sticky** **crown**

Next, he put cameras on the towers. When any dragons came near his castle, an alarm sounded,
beep-beep-beep.
The doors closed,
clunk.
The bridge went up,
creak.
And an automatic message said,

Many castles had big doors that came down when the drawbridge went up.

"Let's have our picnic somewhere else," said the dragons.

Then the king filled the moat with super-sticky glue.
SUPER STICKY
Adding **super**- is like adding very, very. How sticky is the glue?
He went to the top of the tower and looked down. He was very excited.
Ha, ha! I have the best …
But just then, his crown fell off.
It fell down
down
down
onto the bridge
and into the glue.

How do you think the king feels?
The king ran down the stairs …

across the bridge …

and he tried to pull his crown out of the glue.
Suddenly, he heard the alarm *beep-beep-beep*. The doors went *clunk*. The bridge went *creak*.

Then he heard,

I have the best castle.
I'm a clever king.
You can try and try
but you can't come in!

Some words sound like noises, for example, **beep**. Can you find two more in the story?

The king felt sad. He didn't feel clever any more.

Explore the Reading

A Think and complete the story map.

Title: ______________________

Characters

____

Setting

____

Problem

____

Solution

____

B Read and choose the answer.

1. The king is angry / grumpy / kind.
2. The dragons think the king is scary / brave / unfriendly.
3. The king thinks he is funny / clever / friendly.
4. The king thinks his castle is cute / famous / great.
5. At the end of the story, the king is cool / sad / clever.

C Think and discuss. What makes you grumpy? What can you do to feel better?

I'm grumpy when I feel tired.

A Read the questions. Then read quickly and find the answers.

1 Where is the castle?

____

2 How old is the castle?

____

Agra Fort is a very big castle. It is in India. It is 450 years old. It has strong walls and a big bridge.

Sometimes we read to find answers to our questions. When we do this, we can read quickly until we find the answer. This is called **scanning**.

B Scan *Amazing Castles*. Choose one of the castles. Fill in the card.

Name ______________________

How old is it? ______________________

Where is it? ______________________

____

____

____

C Think and discuss. Can you name countries with castles in them?

There are castles in Japan.

Now read **Amazing Castles**

Nonfiction

Amazing Castles

Castles are big, strong buildings. Important people like kings, queens, and emperors built castles to keep their families safe.

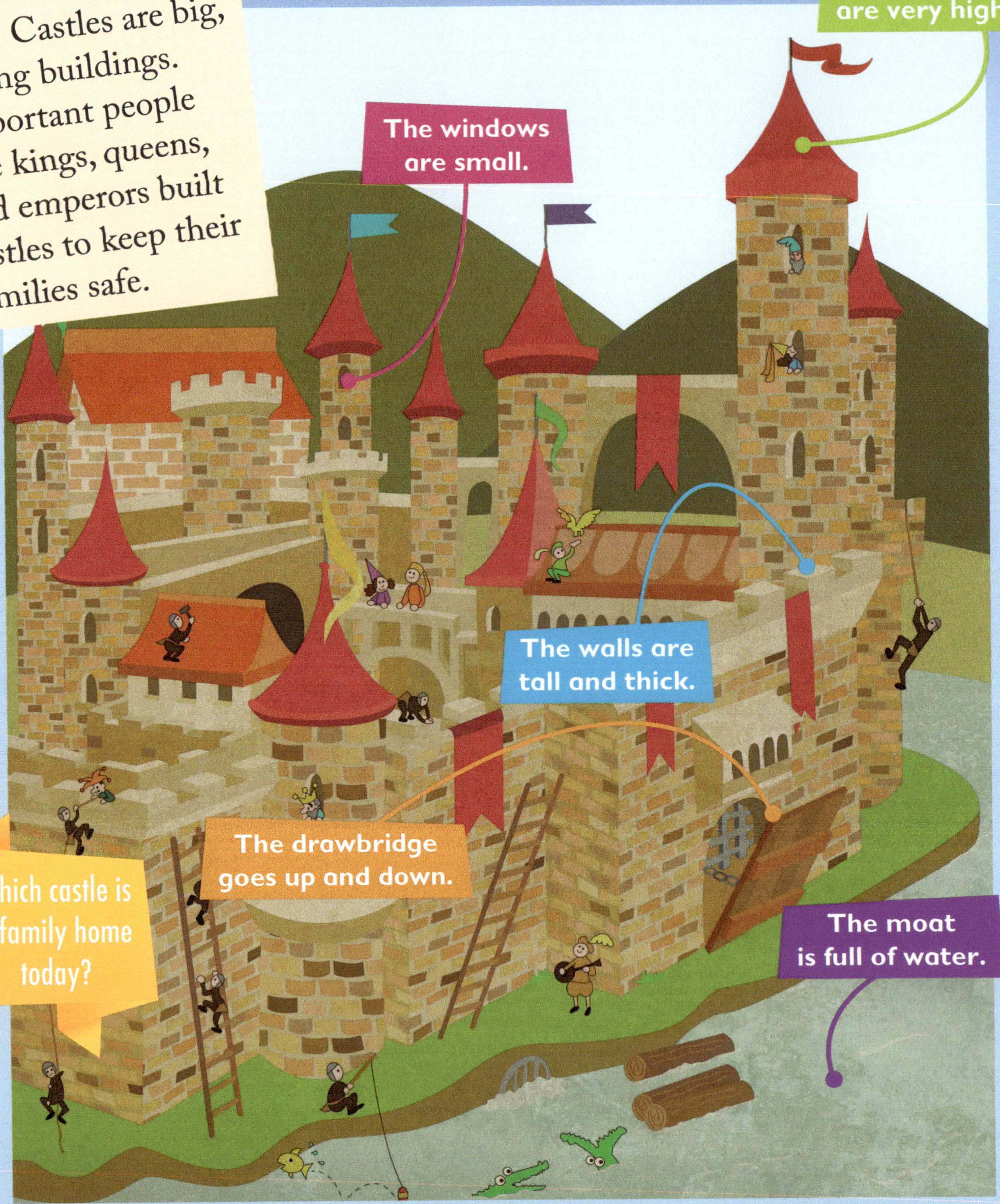

Leeds Castle is in Great Britain. It is about 900 years old. It is on an island in the middle of a lake. The first castle on the island was small. It had wooden walls. King Edward I made the castle stronger. He built high stone walls, and he made the lake bigger. It was his favorite castle. Nobody lives in the castle now.

The names of kings and queens sometimes use Roman numerals. I = 1, II = 2, III = 3, IV = 4, and V = 5

Words in Context

Find these words in the reading. What do you think they mean?

emperors **wooden** **round** **secret** **passages** **bakery** **stables**

Nakhal Fort is more than 1,500 years old. It is in Oman. It is high up on a rock. It has stone walls and a round tower in the middle. Today, there is a museum inside the fort, and every Friday there is a goat market inside the castle walls.

From the top of the tower, visitors can see in all directions. They can see the valley, the mountains, and the palm trees.

The word *fort* means *strong* in Latin.

Brézé Castle is in France. It is about 500 years old. It has a bridge and a big moat, but there's no water in it. Inside the castle there are a lot of rooms to live in. A family still lives in the castle now.

But this castle has a secret …

Under the castle, there is another castle. This is the oldest part of the castle. It is nearly 1,000 years old. There are secret passages and rooms in the rock. Many years ago, there was a kitchen and a bakery for making bread. There were stables for the horses. There was even an ice room for keeping food cool. Nobody lives there now, but people can visit it.

Which castle do you like most? Why?

Explore the Reading

A Look at the picture. Match and write.

windows   moat   walls   towers   door

B Scan the article and find the information. Check (✔) the correct answers.

	Leeds Castle	Nakhal Fort	Brézé Castle
1 This castle is on an island.	✔		
2 This castle is on a rock.			
3 A family lives in a part of this castle today.			
4 This castle has a moat.			
5 There is sometimes a market in this castle.			
6 This castle has rooms underground.			

C Think and discuss. Imagine you can build your own castle. What do you want to use to build it?

> I want to use cheese to build a castle.

Phonics *br–*

Listen and say.

brother   breakfast   brown   Brazil   brain

Now find more words starting with *br–* in the reading.

Why did people build castles?

A Look at your table on page 137. What did you learn about castles?

I Learned that ...
1
2

B Think and discuss. Which castle is the strongest? Why? Do an Inside-Outside Circle.

> I think Brézé Castle is the strongest because it has rooms underground. You can hide.

My Reading Journal

Was there a funny part in this unit? Write or draw about it.

Choose adjectives to describe the unit.

interesting exciting boring fun informative

UNIT 10

Are We There Yet?

See, Think, Wonder

A Look at the picture. What do you see?

I see giraffes.

There's a train.

B What do you think?

They are busy.

I think they are leaving.

C What do you wonder?

How tall are the giraffes?

I wonder where they are going?

D Think and discuss. Did you ever go on a long trip?

1 How long did it take?
2 How did you get there?
3 Did anything funny happen on the way?

E Look, think, and number. What events do you see? What order do you think they happen?

Now read **Young Nicholas**

Fiction

Young Nicholas

October 6, 1769

Dear Diary,

My name's Nicholas. I live on a ship called the *Endeavour*. We're on a journey at sea. We left England a long time ago. Everyone is looking for land. I love the water, but I miss land. I think the other sailors do, too. Everything is blue here.

I'm a cabin boy. Every day, I clean the boat. Today I swept the cabins and scrubbed the deck. Then I saw something swaying in the water. I looked closer. It was a tree branch! I wanted to pull it out, but I couldn't get it. I knew land was close, so I ran to tell the captain.

How does the tree branch tell him land is close?

When I found him, he was talking to his men. "Hear this!" he said. "The first man to find land wins a prize. I'll also name a place after him!"

I'm going to win that prize, I thought. *I'm going to find land.*

Words in Context

Find these words in the reading. What do you think they mean?

ship land branch captain mast

I went to the ship's mast. It was windy, and I climbed up slowly. I kept my eyes on the top of the mast.

Come on, Nicholas! I thought.

At last, I reached the top. From here, I could see a very long way.

I looked and looked. I didn't give up. I needed to find land.

Finally, I saw something. It was very small and far away. My heart started beating faster. I wanted to jump in and swim. There it was—land!

"Land!" I shouted down to the others. "I see land!" Tomorrow, I'm going to get the prize.

I'm so excited!

Yours truly,

Nicholas

Explore the Reading

A Read and answer.

1 What was the name of the ship?

The name of the ship was Endeavour.

2 What were the men looking for?

3 Where did Nicholas see the branch?

4 Why did Nicholas climb the mast?

5 Who won the prize?

B Think and complete the table.

Cause	Effect
1 The ship was close to land.	
2	Nicholas saw land.
3 Nicholas found land first.	

C Think and write. Imagine you are Nicholas. How do you feel?

1 In the beginning, I feel ________________.

2 At the end, I feel ________________.

Phonics *sw–*

Listen and say.

sweater swan swing swap sweet

Now find more words starting with *sw–* in the reading.

A **Read and number. Put the events in order.**

1 The men looked for new land.

☐ "I see land!" said Nicholas.

☐ Nicholas saw a branch in the water.

☐ "The first man to find land wins a prize," said the captain.

☐ Nicholas climbed to the top of the mast.

A sequence is an order. The **sequence of events** is the order that events happen. They help us understand the beginning, middle, and end in a story.

B **Look and number. What is the sequence of events?**

☐

1

☐

☐

☐

C **Think and discuss. Do you think the journey looks easy? Why or why not?**

No, I don't think so. He doesn't have a car.

Now read **The Thirty-Year Journey**

Nonfiction

THE THIRTY-YEAR JOURNEY

Ibn Battuta was one of the world's greatest travelers. He was born in Morocco in 1304. Ibn Battuta left his home when he was 21 years old. He went on a journey that took 30 years! He wanted to learn about the world. He saw more of the world than anyone else in his time.

When he started his journey, Ibn Battuta was all by himself.

What words describe the main character?

Later, Ibn Battuta traveled through the desert with caravans. They rode their animals, cooked, and camped together. Some caravans had thousands of people. They were almost like a moving town.

Words in Context

Find these words in the reading. What do you think they mean?

travelers caravans camped dangers robbed ruler

Traveling in those days was hard. There were many dangers on the road. Once, Ibn Battuta was robbed and left with only his clothes. Sometimes, he had to run for his life!

What do you think *run for his life* means?

Traveling by ship was hard, too. There were big storms with thunder and lightning.

Ibn Battuta traveled more than 120,000 km.!

Ibn Battuta wanted to see everything. He traveled through deserts, across seas, and over mountains. He traveled through Africa and into parts of Europe. He also went to the Middle East and India. He even went to Southeast Asia and China.

He missed his home and went back to Morocco. The ruler of Morocco wanted to hear all about his journey. Ibn Battuta told his stories to a writer, and together they wrote a book called *Ar-Rihla*. In the book, Ibn Battuta describes all the people and places he saw. The book gives us a good idea of life in those days.

Rihla means **journey** in Arabic. Have you ever taken a journey?

Today, to remember him and his great journey, there is a place on the moon called Ibn Battuta.

Explore the Reading

A Look and number. Put the events in order.

B Read and match. How do you think Ibn Battuta feels?

1 He leaves home.

2 He travels with a caravan.

3 He is robbed.

4 He tells his story.

excited

scared

proud

happy

C Think and write. Why does Ibn Battuta keep traveling for 30 years? Write three reasons.

1 ______

2 ______

3 ______

Why do people travel?

A Work with a group. Make a Venn diagram about Nicholas and Ibn Battuta.

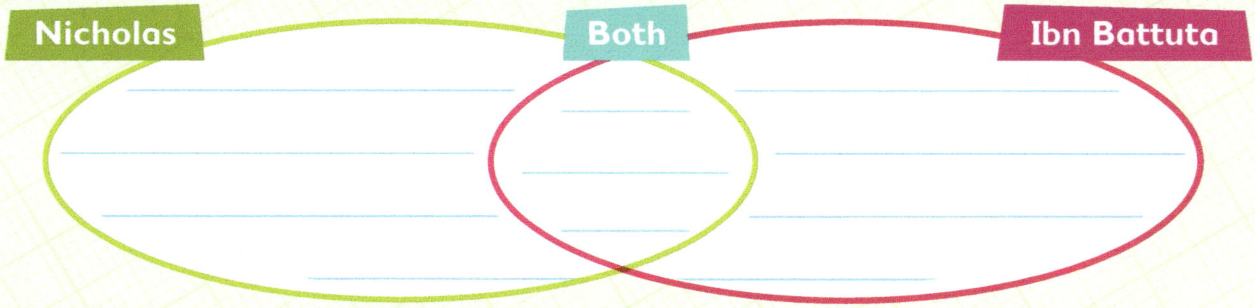

B Think and write. Imagine you're going on a journey like Nicholas and Ibn Battuta. Where do you want to go? Why?

I want to go to ______ *because* ______
______.

C Think and discuss. Where do you want to travel? Why? Do a Three-step Interview and talk about it.

Where do you want to travel?

I want to go to Costa Rica.

Alexa wants to go to Costa Rica.

My Reading Journal

For each compass direction, write down a fun fact from the unit. Can you find four things you found interesting?

N ______

W ______ E ______

S ______

How can you learn more about famous journeys?

I can learn more by ______.

Macmillan Education
4 Crinan Street
London N1 9XW
A division of Springer Nature Limited

Companies and representatives throughout the world

Literacy Book ISBN 978-1-786-32348-4
Student Book Pack ISBN 978-1-380-00224-2

Written by Paul Mason, Nicole Taylor, and Michael Watts

First published 2019

Original design by D'Sign Lab
Page make-up by D'Sign Lab
Illustrated by Carles Arbat (MB Artists) pp. 74–79, 81; Beatrice Bencivenni (Beehive Illustration) p. 127; Mariona Cabassas (MB Artists) pp. 26, 30; Emmanuel Cerisier (Beehive Illustration) pp. 160–166; Moreno Chiacchiera (Beehive Illustration) pp. 154–157, 159; Maine Diaz (MB Artists) pp. 112–119, 127; D'Sign Lab pp. 10–21, 49–51, 54, 82, 99, 134, 146; Gary Hanna (Lemonade Illustration Agency) pp. 105–110; Daniela Geremia (Beehive Illustration) pp. 24–25; Emi Ordás pp. 4, 6; Macky Pamintuan (MB Artists) pp. 57–63; Rémy Simard (MB Artists) pp. 10–15, 17, 31, 65; Jomike Tejido (MB Artists) pp. 90–96, 111; Francois Ruyer (Beehive Illustration) pp. 152–153; Felipe Van Rompaey (Lemonade Illustration Agency) pp. 121–133, 135, 13–143; Donald Wu (MB Artists) pp. 31–39, 65; Jennifer Zivoin (MB Artists) pp. 41–45, 47, 65, 66–69.

Front cover design and concept by 3CD
Cover adaptation by Roberto Martinez
Cover illustration by Jennifer Zivoin
Cover photograph by Getty Images/Leonello Calvetti/Stocktrek Images (globe)
Picture research by Emily Taylor

Authors' acknowledgements
Paul Mason:
I would like to acknowledge and thank the team at Macmillan and RedNova Learning. Working together was a privilege.

Nicole Taylor and Michael Watts:
We would like to thank our co-authors for their input and creativity and the editorial team at Macmillan and RedNova Learning for all their support. It has been a pleasure to work on this project.

The publishers would like to thank: Colegio Buckingham and Gabriela Rodriguez, Colegio Euterpe and Angélica Sánchez, Colegio Heroes Mexicanos and Marcelo Carlos Hernández Morales, Internaciones Campus Fraijanes and Ana Monica Thomas, New Victoria International College and Ghada Hassan Mokbel, The Southern Cross School and Dayana Acevedo, Antonia Lira, and Paula Jorquera, Verbo Quetzaltenango and Cindy Steicy Ixchiu Velásquez, Salwa Abid, Riham Almughrabi, Maria Pia Ayala, Meryem Bennis, Leticia Blazquez, Angel Bonilla, Victor Cojulun, John Cruft, Silvia Díez de Rivera, Randa Farouk, Magda Giomazi, Vangelina Hernandez, Quyen Ho, Ziad Jadallah, Youngkwang Jang, Faisal M'reish, Jackie Mustoe, Adriana Ochoa, Devrim Ozdemir, Silvia Raya, Ola Refaat, Jacqueline Sabri, Helen Sharbain, Sana Sifri, Susan Thornhill, Esra Tosun, Lemmy Trujillo, Tamer Victor, Jake Whiddon, Sandra Wu, Amanda Zhang.

The authors and publishers would like to thank the following for permission to reproduce their photographs: **Alamy**/EPA p. 29, Alamy/Martyn Evans p. 19(shoes), Alamy/Granger Historical Picture Archive pp. 56–57, Alamy/Heritage Image Partnership Ltd p. 98(tr), Alamy/Hi–Story p. 21, Alamy/Image Republic Inc pp. 25, 27, Alamy/JeongHyeon Noh p. 28(top), Alamy/Electra kay–smith p. 102(b), Alamy/Keystone Pictures USA p. 122(bl, t), Alamy/ITAR-TASS Photo Agency p. 122(br), Alamy/Nino Marcutti p. 103, Alamy/J Marshall-Tribaleye Images p. 84(bl), Alamy/MBI p. 48(tm), Alamy/Pictorial Press Ltd p. 126, Alamy/Really Easy Star/Selina Bressan pp. 145(background), 148(b), Alamy/REUTERS p. 83(t, bl), Alamy/Scenicireland.com/Christopher Hill Photographic pp. 97(background), 99, 102(2), Alamy/Lucas Vallecillos pp. 101(b), 102(5), Alamy/Wenn Ltd pp. 47(background), 52, Alamy/Zoonar GmbH p. 98(b); **Bluwave Creative**/Johnson-Dailey p. 19(old & new); **Getty Images**/AFP p. 53, Images/Robert Albert p. 28(bottom), Getty Images/Bettmann Archive p. 125, Getty Images/Blend Images p. 48(tl), Getty Images/Biosphoto p. 102(d), Getty Images/Central Press pp. 124, 127, Getty Images/Gary S. Chapman p. 102(c), Getty Images/Ashley Cooper p. 40–41, Getty Images/De Agostini p. 148(t), Getty Images/Dorling Kindersley p. 19(foot), Getty Images/EyeEm pp. 48–49(background), Getty Images/Rick Friedman/Corbis p. 83(br), Getty Images/Gamma-Keystone p. 127, Getty Images/Hemera pp. 17(pencils), 20(pencils), Getty Images/Dave G. Houser pp. 100(br), 102(4), Getty Images/Hulton Archive pp. 20(tr), 123, 126, Getty Images/iStockphoto pp. 47(l, r), 100(t, cl), 102(1,3), Getty Images/Domingo Leiva p. 101(tr), Getty Images/Mondadori p. 18(Edison), Getty Images/Bruno Morandi p. 149(t), Getty Images/National Geographic Magazines p. 19(kingfisher), Getty Images/Photodisc p. 48(tr), Getty Images/Martin Pickard p. 51(t), Getty Images/Alex Spatari p. 19(train), Getty Images/Stocktrek Images pp. 81(background), 84–85(background); **PlainPicture**/Neuebildanstalt/Burkart pp. 72–73(background); **Rex Features**/Magic Car Pics/REX/Shutterstock p. 51(b); **Shutterstock/Dr Flash** pp. 88–89, **Shutterstock**/imagedb.com p. 145, Shutterstock/Philip Lange pp. 136–137, Shutterstock/Stephen Mulligan p. 147, Shutterstock/NataLT pp. 17(background), 18–19(background), 20(background), Shutterstock/Nel727 p. 102(e), Shutterstock/sNike p. 102(a), Shutterstock/Offset/Tom Stahl pp. 104–105, Shutterstock/Passakorn sakulphan pp. 17(pens), p. 20(pens), Shutterstock/Svinkin p. 47(bottom), Shutterstock/Taigi pp. 5–6(background), 6–7(background), 23(background), 39(background), 55, 71(background), 87(background), 103(background), 119(background), 135(background), 151(background), 167(background), Shutterstock/Vasilyev Alexandr pp. 8–9; **UN Photo**/Yutaka Nagata p. 85(tl), UN Photo/Rice p. 85(mr), UN Photo/B Wolff p. 85(bl).

Commissioned photographs by Luise Johnson-Dailey, Bluwave Creative p. 19(old & new)

Printed and bound in Uruguay

2023
35